Lectionary for Masses with Children

Year A

APPROVED FOR USE IN THE
DIOCESES OF THE UNITED STATES OF AMERICA
BY THE NATIONAL CONFERENCE OF CATHOLIC BISHOPS
AND CONFIRMED BY THE APOSTOLIC SEE

PREPARED BY THE COMMITTEE ON THE LITURGY
NATIONAL CONFERENCE OF CATHOLIC BISHOPS

Concordat cum originali:

> Robert N. Lynch
> General Secretary
> National Conference of Catholic Bishops

Published by authority of the Committee on the Liturgy, National Conference of Catholic Bishops.

ACKNOWLEDGMENTS

Readings from the Old Testament, New Testament, Book of Psalms, and a select number of the refrains for the responsorial psalms are taken from the *Contemporary English Version*, copyright © 1991 by the American Bible Society, 1875 Broadway, New York, N.Y. 10023, and are used by license of the American Bible Society. All rights reserved.

The compilation of the *Lectionary for Masses with Children* and introduction, copyright © 1992, United States Catholic Conference, Inc., 3211 Fourth Street, NE, Washington, DC 20017-1194, is used by license of said copyright owner. All rights reserved. No part of the *Lectionary for Masses with Children* may be reproduced in any form without permission in writing from the copyright owner.

The English translation of the titles of the readings, psalm responses, Alleluia verses, Lenten acclamations and verses before the gospel from the *Lectionary for Mass*, copyright © 1969, 1980, 1982, and 1992, International Committee on English in the Liturgy, Inc. (ICEL), 1275 K Street, NW, Washington, DC 20005-4097. All rights reserved.

05 04 03 02 01 00 99 98   7 6 5 4 3

Copyright © 1994, Archdiocese of Chicago. All rights reserved. Liturgy Training Publications, 1800 North Hermitage Avenue, Chicago IL 60622-1101; 1-800-933-1800; fax 1-800-933-7094; e-mail orders@ltp.org.

Editor: David A. Lysik
Copy Editor: Theresa Pincich
Designer: Kerry Perlmutter
Typesetter: Mark Hollopeter
Artist: Steve Erspamer, SM

ISBN 1-56854-000-0
CLA/SE

NATIONAL CONFERENCE OF CATHOLIC BISHOPS
UNITED STATES OF AMERICA

DECREE

The *Lectionary for Masses with Children* for use in the dioceses of the United States of America was canonically approved by the members of the National Conference of Catholic Bishops on 13 November 1991 and was subsequently confirmed by the Apostolic See by decree of the Congregation for Divine Worship and the Discipline of the Sacraments on 27 May 1992 (Prot. N. 1259/91).

As of 1 September 1993 the *Lectionary for Masses with Children* may be published and used in the liturgy. The First Sunday of Advent, 28 November 1993, is hereby established as the effective date for use of the *Lectionary for Masses with Children* in the dioceses of the United States of America. From that day forward no other English lectionary for Masses with children may be used.

Given at the General Secretariat of the National Conference of Catholic Bishops, Washington DC, on 28 December 1992, the feast of the Holy Innocents.

    + William H. Keeler
       Archbishop of Baltimore
       President
       National Conference of Catholic Bishops

       Robert N. Lynch
       General Secretary

CONGREGATION FOR DIVINE WORSHIP AND THE DISCIPLINE OF THE SACRAMENTS

Prot. N. 1259/91

This Congregation has examined the request of the National Conference of Catholic Bishops of the United States of America for the confirmation of the approval for the *Lectionary for Masses with Children*.

We grant permission for the experimental use of the cursus of the lectionary for children. After a three-year period a full report of the experiment must be given and a renewal or definitive confirmation will be given.

The terms of the permission are as follows:

1. We ask that it be established as a first principle what is stated in paragraph 13 of the Introduction to the *Lectionary for Masses with Children*:

    "Proper balance and consideration for the entire assembly should be observed. Therefore, priest celebrants should not use this *Lectionary for Masses with Children* exclusively or even preferentially at Sunday Masses, even though large numbers of children are present."

2. a. In granting permission for the cursus to be used, independently of any approved version of the Scripture, no approved version is *a priori* excluded from use. However, there is one small modification regarding the cursus.

    b. Before the readings for the following celebrations, Christmas Day, Epiphany, Sundays of Lent, Easter Sunday, Ascension, and Pentecost, it is asked that a rubric be added stating that, "these readings may be used only when the celebration of the liturgy of the word for the children is held in a place apart from the main assembly." This is to ensure that on these days in the assembly the universal lectionary will take precedence over the children's lectionary.

3. On the basis of the assurance given that the *Contemporary English Version* of the Bible does not present any doctrinal problems in the sphere of the issue of the inclusive language question at present under study we grant permission for its experimental use but without granting a formal confirmation.

From the Congregation for Divine Worship and the Discipline of the Sacraments, 27 May 1992.

    +   Antonio María Cardinal Javierre Ortas
           Prefect

    +   Geraldo M. Agnelo
           Archbishop Secretary

CONTENTS

Decree of the National Conference of Catholic Bishops	*iii*
Decree of the Congregation for Divine Worship and the Discipline of the Sacraments	*iv*
Foreword	*vi*
Introduction	*viii*

Proper of Seasons	
Season of Advent	*1*
Season of Christmas	*19*
Season of Lent	*41*
Season of Easter	*77*
Ordinary Time	*115*

Solemnities of the Lord during Ordinary Time	*253*
Common Texts for Responsorial Psalms	*267*
Calendar	*284*
Index of Readings	*294*

FOREWORD

Throughout his ministry, our Lord Jesus Christ had a special concern for children. When his disciples tried to prevent parents from bringing their children to Jesus to bless them, the Lord became angry and reminded the disciples: "Let the children come to me! Don't try to stop them. People who are like these little children belong to the kingdom of God" (Mk 10:14). The Gospels record other incidences when Jesus healed sick children and even raised them to life (e.g., Lk 8:40 – 56, Lk 9:37 – 43, Mt 17:14 – 18, Mk 9:14 – 27).

The Church too has manifested a special care and concern for children through the ages. From the time an infant is baptized the Church seeks to enfold it in its loving embrace so that the child may grow in the love of God. Parents are reminded: "It will be your duty to bring [your child] up to keep God's commandments as Christ taught us, by loving God and our neighbor." And in response to their affirmative answer, the minister addresses the child and says: "N., the Christian community welcomes you with great joy. In its name I claim you for Christ our Savior by the sign of his cross." The welcome of children by the Church must not be a one-time event; rather, the Church, in following the example of Christ, continues to welcome all children, but especially the young, into its midst and into its liturgical assemblies.

A concrete expression of the Church's concern for the pastoral care of children is found in the *Directory for Masses with Children*, published by the Congregation for Divine Worship in 1973 as a supplement to the *General Instruction of the Roman Missal*. This document provides for adaptations that can be made when the eucharist is celebrated with young children so that the words and actions of the Mass will be more suitable to the comprehension of the children. The Directory, in particular, provides for the adaptation of the liturgy of the word and recommends that individual conferences of bishops see to the composition of lectionaries for Masses with children.

At the recommendation of the Federation of Diocesan Liturgical Commissions and with its assistance, the Committee on the Liturgy of the National Conference of Catholic Bishops undertook the project of preparing a children's lectionary for Mass. The task group responsible for this work compared the existing lectionaries for children in other languages and, always keeping an eye on the Roman *Lectionary for Mass*, elaborated the *cursus* of readings that is found in this *Lectionary for Masses with Children* and prepared the introduction to the Lectionary. The work of the task group, which consisted of experts in liturgy, scripture, and catechetics, was ultimately approved by the NCCB Liturgy Committee and by the entire National Conference of Catholic Bishops. The Congregation for Divine Worship and the Discipline of the Sacraments has approved the

Lectionary for Masses with Children for experimental use for a period of three years at which time the approval will be renewed or a definitive decree of confirmation will be granted.

The *Lectionary for Masses with Children* is principally intended for use at Masses which are primarily for children and not the ordinary Sunday Mass. "Proper balance and consideration for the entire assembly should be observed. Therefore, priest celebrants should not use this *Lectionary for Masses with Children* exclusively or even preferentially at Sunday Masses, even though large numbers of children are present" (Introduction, no. 13).

It is the hope of the Liturgy Committee that the *Lectionary for Masses with Children* will enable children to hear the word of God in a manner more suited to their age and ability to understand. In providing this lectionary it is our sincere desire to enable young children to come to Christ, from whom they have received new life in baptism and who gives them the joy of salvation.

+ Wilton D. Gregory
Auxiliary Bishop of Chicago
Chairman, Committee on the Liturgy
National Conference of Catholic Bishops

INTRODUCTION

I. The Liturgical Celebration of the Word of God

LIVING WORD OF GOD

1. God speaks to us the Word, who has become flesh in Jesus Christ our Lord. Through him all things came to be and were made.[1] The many words spoken throughout history for our salvation have their origin and end in Christ Jesus.[2] In the liturgy we are called together that in the Spirit we may listen to and respond to the word of God in Christ. "That word constantly proclaimed in the liturgy is always, then, a living, active word through the power of the Holy Spirit. It expresses the Father's love that never fails in its effectiveness toward us."[3]

WORD OF GOD IN THE ASSEMBLY

2. The liturgical assembly is a gathering of God's holy People. Christ is present in the very act of gathering.[4] Christ is also present in the proclamation of the word of God.[5] This proclamation, if it is to promote a deeper experience of Christ's presence, must be understood in its most complete sense. It must be prepared for and experienced as the specific kind of event it is, namely, a ritual celebration composed of reading, dialogue in song, silence, and reflection, with the use of appropriate gestures and symbols. The ability to give assent to God's Good News is deeply influenced by the manner in which the word is proclaimed and celebrated in the liturgical assembly.[6] The Church's deepest calling is to praise God. Members of the Church do this by conforming their lives to the message of the Scriptures that they have heard and by bringing to the celebration of the liturgy all that they have done.[7]

GOD'S WORD IN STORY

3. Christian communities discover, express, and deepen their identity by sharing the stories of our salvation that we read in the Scriptures. The way we pass these biblical stories on to children will also influence the way in which the message of the Scriptures is communicated to the children.

LITURGY OF THE WORD

4. One of the clearest aims and achievements of the liturgical reform after the Second Vatican Council has been the renewal of the scriptural elements of liturgical prayer and the wider opening of the Scriptures within the full cycle of liturgical seasons and celebrations.[8] Every sacramental rite, blessing, and hour of prayer calls for the proclamation of the word of God in the form of a liturgy of the word. The most effective realization of this proclamation is the eucharist, the visible word or sacrament of the paschal mystery into which we have been baptized. Full nourishment comes from the tables of God's word and eucharist.[9]

LITURGICAL MINISTRIES

5. In its liturgy the Christian community acts in its capacity as an "ordered diversity of members" and ministries.[10] The liturgy is a dialogue between God and the Church. This dialogue is effected by the Spirit's activity

informing and inspiring the coordinated ministry of all who form the liturgical assembly (children as well as adults, including its bishops, presbyters, deacons, readers, musicians, and acolytes).[11]

II. The Celebration of the Word of God with Children

SCRIPTURE NEVER OMITTED
6. The Directory for Masses with Children clearly sets forth the Church's desire that children, no less than other members of the community, be formed by the same word of God. Therefore, at Masses with adults in which children also participate and at Masses with children in which only a few adults participate "biblical reading should never be omitted."[12]

SEPARATE LITURGY OF THE WORD
7. In Masses with adults in which children also participate, "[s]ometimes, moreover, if the place itself and the nature of the community permit, it will be appropriate to celebrate the liturgy of the word, including a homily, with the children in a separate, but not too distant, room."[13]

8. When children are to participate in the liturgy of the word in a space separate from the main assembly, they first gather with the rest of the assembly to celebrate the introductory rites. At the conclusion of the opening prayer, but before the first reading is proclaimed, the presiding priest may formally send the children and their ministers to the place where they will celebrate their own liturgy of the word. This may be done by presenting the Lectionary to the one who will preside over the liturgy of the word with the children and/or by words of dismissal, such as the following:

A Receive this book of readings
and proclaim God's word faithfully
to the children entrusted to your care.

B My dear children,
you will now go to hear God's word,
to praise God in song,
and to reflect on the wonderful things God has done for us.
We will await your return
so that together we may celebrate the eucharist.

At the conclusion of their liturgy of the word, and before the liturgy of the eucharist begins, the children return to their families.

WEEKDAY MASSES WITH CHILDREN
9. Although children are always to be led toward the parish's Sunday celebration of the eucharist, nevertheless, during the week Masses with children in which only a few adults participate are recommended.[14]

HOMILY OR EXPLANATION OF THE READINGS
10. Because the explanation of the Scripture readings is so important at Masses with children, a homily should always be given. However, in order that they may not be deprived of the riches of God's word, especially if the priest finds it difficult to adapt himself to the mentality of children, and

with the consent of the pastor or rector of the church, one of the adults participating in these celebrations may speak to the children after the gospel.[15]

III. The Lectionary for Masses with Children

A. One Lectionary

PURPOSE OF ADAPTATION
11. This *Lectionary for Masses with Children* adheres as closely as possible to the selection and arrangement of readings for Sundays, solemnities, and feasts of the Lord in the *Lectionary for Mass*, while adapting them to the needs and capacities of children. In adapting the liturgy for use with children, the Church's goal is to nourish their faith and lead them to "active, conscious, and authentic" participation in the worship of the whole assembly,[16] but not to establish a different rite for children.[17]

USE OF THIS LECTIONARY
12. In providing a lectionary for celebrations of the eucharist in which a considerable number of children are present, the Church intends to lead them into one community of faith, formed by the proclamation of the word of God. The scriptural readings contained in this Lectionary may be used at Sunday Masses when a large number of children are present along with adults, or when the children have a separate liturgy of the word, or for Masses at which most of the congregation consists of children (e.g., school Masses). The readings of this Lectionary are also a useful resource for those who wish to prepare other liturgical celebrations with children, and wish to do so within the context of the liturgical year.

13. Proper balance and consideration for the entire assembly should be observed. Therefore, priest celebrants should not use this *Lectionary for Masses with Children* exclusively or even preferentially at Sunday Masses, even though large numbers of children are present. In addition, this Lectionary may be used only when the liturgy of the word with the children is held in a place apart from the main assembly on Christmas Day, Epiphany, the Sundays of Lent, Easter Day, Ascension, and Pentecost. This is to ensure that on these days the Roman *Lectionary for Mass* will take precedence over the *Lectionary for Masses with Children* in the main assembly of the faithful.[18]

FAMILY PREPARATION
14. Although the Church permits the liturgy of the word to be celebrated in a place apart from the main Sunday assembly,[19] it seeks to protect and foster the domestic church which is the Christian family.[20] This might be weakened if all the Scripture readings heard by parents were substantially different from those heard by their children on the same Sunday. This Lectionary is intended to encourage families to prepare together those readings which will be used in common both by the adults and the children for the celebration of the Sunday Mass (at least the gospel) and to reflect after the celebration on the word proclaimed there.

B. Adapted for Particular Hearers of the Word

AGE LEVEL
15. The hearers of the word for whom this work is primarily intended are children of elementary grades [preadolescents].[21]

NUMBER OF READINGS
16. "If three or even two readings appointed on Sundays or weekdays can be understood by children only with difficulty, it is permissible to read two or only one of them, but the reading of the gospel should never be omitted."[22]

OMISSION OF READINGS
17. In the preparation of this Lectionary, readings from the *Lectionary for Mass* which were judged to be too abstract were eliminated or shortened.[23] Also omitted were passages of Scripture containing images that could confuse or disturb children, or readings children could perceive as anti-Semitic or racist.[24]

LENGTH OF READINGS
18. Length was not the sole criterion for elimination or abridgment.[25] In particular cases longer or shorter forms of readings have been provided. Liturgical planners, with the consent of the priest celebrant, may further adapt particularly long readings by choosing to use only that part of the selection which presents a particular biblical image or is directly related to the other reading(s).

REPLACEMENT OF READINGS
19. When one of the first two readings for Sundays or solemnities or feasts of the Lord was judged inappropriate for children, it was omitted and not replaced with another. In cases where both of the two first readings in the Lectionary have been dropped, a replacement has been provided. The gospel selections appointed in the Roman *Lectionary for Mass* have been retained although in particular cases they have been shortened or otherwise adapted.

RESPONSORIAL PSALMS
20. The responsorial psalms of the Lectionary have been adapted in order to foster the singing of these texts.[26] Some refrains and psalms have been shortened or replaced. For the most part, the responsorial psalms are related to the first reading.[27] To make it easier for the assembly to join in singing the responsorial psalm, some common texts have been provided for the liturgical seasons and for the commons of saints. These may be used in place of the assigned responsorial psalms when they are sung.[28]

C. That the Word of God Might Be Proclaimed in the Liturgical Celebration

WORTHY CELEBRATION
21. The liturgy has the power to form children and all believers in the paschal mystery. The worthy celebration of the liturgy itself is the best introduction to liturgy.[29]

BODILY INVOLVEMENT
22. In order to engage children's authentic participation, liturgy must respect their need for physical involvement. They should be invited to participate in the actions of the liturgy whenever it is appropriate and possible.[30] Their internal life is still very much dependent upon what they experience through their senses. Therefore, ritual elements such as gestures and postures, processions, song, dialogue, silence, and the use of symbols are integral to their experience of the liturgy.

MINISTERS
23. Children imitate the behaviors and attitudes of adults. For this reason, adults who serve as ministers at liturgical celebrations where children are present should conduct the entire range of liturgical actions, gestures, and songs with dignity and care, yet without becoming distant or mechanical. All liturgical ministries are exercised for the sake of the prayer of the assembly. Therefore, ministers should be selected on the basis of liturgical competence. It should not be presumed that children should proclaim the word of God in the celebrations in which this Lectionary is used. Some younger children are able to read the Scriptures competently, but the witness of older children, teenagers, or adults, ministering graciously and reverently to young children engaged in liturgical prayer, is more conducive to the children's growing reverence for the word of God, than the peer ministry of embarrassed or ill-prepared children.[31]

RITUAL PRAYER
24. The Church's liturgy is first and foremost ritual prayer. The liturgy of the word is neither a catechetical session nor an introduction to biblical history. The liturgy celebrates the word of God in narrative and song, makes it visible in gesture and symbol and culminates in the celebration of the eucharist.

D. Throughout the Liturgical Year

INTRODUCTION: CALENDARS EXPRESS AND SHAPE IDENTITY
25. A calendar marks the celebrations which shape, carry on and expand a particular community's common life. This Lectionary, like the Roman *Lectionary for Mass* of which it is an adaptation, is based on the Church's calendar called the liturgical year. Its faithful observance is vital to Catholic identity. This is true for children no less than for adults. Faithful observance of the calendar promotes formation and participation in the life of the Church.

PASCHAL MYSTERY
26. The Sundays, seasons and feasts of the liturgical year celebrate many facets of a single mystery. Each of them expresses from a different perspective the one great mystery of Christ's dying and rising yesterday, today and for ever. The mystery of redemption effected by Christ's incarnation, death, and resurrection is grounded in historical events of the past, yet leads to a future glory not yet fully revealed. The entire mystery, however, is present: God is now creating and redeeming in Christ. Each day Christ's Church is dying and coming to new life in him through the indwelling of the Spirit given at baptism. In ritual prayer, past and future are caught up into God's

eternal present. Hence the liturgy is not an historical pageant trying to recreate a long-past event but rather is a true participation in Christ's death and resurrection, the paschal mystery. An understanding and appropriation of this mystery provides the essential starting point for preparing and celebrating the Church's liturgy.

SUNDAY

27. The shaping of time in the Church's tradition is related to the rhythms of nature, e.g., the relationship of morning and evening prayer to the daily rising and setting of the sun. The most fundamental shape of liturgical time, however, is the week. The first day of the week, Sunday, is the Lord's Day on which Christians assemble to celebrate the paschal mystery whose fullest expression is the celebration of the eucharist. Although it may be possible in appropriate ways to integrate a civil, diocesan, parochial, or domestic celebration within the Sunday liturgy, the full assembly's celebration of the Sunday eucharist must always take precedence over other special occasions. Fidelity to the Lectionary on Sundays, whether during the seasons or in Ordinary Time, is an indispensable element of Catholic formation. This Lectionary contains the readings for all the Sundays of the liturgical year in each year of the three-year cycle of readings.

WEEKDAYS

28. In addition to the readings for Sunday, this Lectionary provides thirty-six sets of readings for the weekdays in Ordinary Time. All four gospels are represented in these weekday selections. The readings provided for the weekdays of each season are generally taken from the respective Sundays and weekdays of the *Lectionary for Mass* so that the images fundamental to the understanding and celebration of that season are adequately represented. Each set of readings has a heading which points out the dominant theme of the readings.

THE SEASONS: EASTER TRIDUUM, SEASON OF EASTER, AND SEASON OF LENT

29. THE TRIDUUM. The Easter Triduum or three days "begins with the evening Mass of the Lord's Supper on Holy Thursday, reaches its high point in the Easter Vigil, and closes with evening prayer on Easter Sunday."[32] The Sunday by Sunday celebration of our life in Christ finds its culmination in this annual celebration of Christ's passover from death to new life. These three days are best understood and celebrated as one liturgy which in its totality celebrates the paschal mystery. The liturgies of each day highlight the different facets of this mystery.

30. The duplication of the liturgies of Holy Thursday and Good Friday is permitted only with the permission of the Ordinary and, in the case of the Easter Vigil, is prohibited. These liturgies have a power and simplicity all of their own. No provision is made for a separate liturgy of the word for children on these occasions and this Lectionary has not provided adapted readings for these occasions. Nevertheless, care should be taken to ensure that participation by children in these celebrations is both encouraged and fostered.

31. The united proclamation of Christ's death and resurrection first sounds in the entrance song of the Evening Mass of the Lord's Supper: "We should glory in the cross of our Lord Jesus Christ, for he is our salvation, our life and our resurrection; through him we are saved and made free."[33] It intensifies in the antiphon at the veneration of the cross on Good Friday: "We worship you, Lord, we venerate your cross, we praise your resurrection. Through the cross you brought joy to the world." It climaxes in the Easter Vigil Preface: "We praise you with greater joy than ever on this Easter night when Christ became our paschal sacrifice." It echoes in the reading for Evening Prayer of Easter Sunday, the closing liturgy of the Triduum: "Christ has offered one single sacrifice for sins. . . . By virtue of that one single offering he has achieved the eternal perfection of all whom he is sanctifying."[34]

32. The Easter Triduum should reflect our deepest belief that Christ has died once for all and that Holy Thursday evening, Good Friday and Holy Saturday are as much celebrations of the Lord's paschal mystery as is Easter Sunday, although each of these days may focus upon a particular aspect of that mystery which cannot be separated from the others.

33. THE SEASON OF EASTER. Following ancient tradition, the Church celebrates Easter for fifty days, from Easter Sunday to Pentecost. These fifty days are understood to be and are celebrated as one "great Sunday."[35] The Scripture readings, liturgical texts, and rites of these fifty days take precedence over civil, school, diocesan, parochial, or domestic celebrations. These events may be integrated with the celebration of the season of Easter, but this should be done with great care.

34. The primacy of the celebration of the Sundays of Easter is rooted in the traditional character of this period as a time for ongoing catechesis, especially in regard to the sacraments of initiation (baptism, confirmation, and eucharist) and to the deeper spiritual meaning of the liturgical rites. This particular expression of the Church's formation process is called mystagogy.[36] Since most children have been baptized as infants and have received or soon will receive the eucharist, it is appropriate to draw out the meaning of these initiatory sacraments for the children during this season.

35. Throughout the season of Easter the first reading is from the Acts of the Apostles. In a three-year cycle of parallel and progressive selections, material is presented on the life of the primitive Church, its witness and growth.[37] For the second reading, passages are taken from I Peter in Year A, I John in Year B, the Revelation of John in Year C. "These are the texts that seem to fit in especially well with the spirit of joyous faith and sure hope proper to this season."[38] The gospel selections for the first three Sundays of Easter recount the appearances of the risen Christ. On the Fourth Sunday, the gospel is that of the Good Shepherd; on the Fifth, Sixth, and Seventh Sundays the Lord's discourse and prayer at the Last Supper are read. Eight sets of readings are provided for the weekdays of the Easter season.

36. THE SEASON OF LENT. Lent extends from Ash Wednesday until just before the Holy Thursday Mass of the Lord's Supper. This season is a period of preparation for the celebration of the Easter Triduum.

37. The season of Lent takes its shape and meaning from the process and rites of conversion which lead to baptism. The process of initiation gave birth to the forty days of Lent. The privileged nature of the Triduum and the joyous celebration of Easter for fifty days can be adequately understood and maintained in worship only if Lent has led the community to the realization that this season celebrates the very nature of Christian life. As catechumens are enrolled on the First Sunday of Lent for baptism at the Easter Vigil, the word of God calls all Christians — children as well as adults — back to a deeper appreciation of their own baptism.

38. The readings, prayers, and Lenten seasonal practices are ultimately to be interpreted and celebrated in the light of our baptism into Christ's dying and rising. The gospels for the first two Sundays of Lent in all three cycles recount the Lord's temptation and transfiguration. The readings of Year A for the Third, Fourth, and Fifth Sundays of Lent are of major importance to Christian initiation and are always used when the Scrutinies are celebrated and may also be used in Years B and C even when there are no catechumens in the parish. "The Old Testament readings are about the history of salvation, which is one of the themes proper to the catechesis of Lent. The series of texts for each year presents the main elements of salvation history from its beginning until the promise of the New Covenant."[39] For the season of Lent only three selections from the letters of the apostles are included in this Lectionary. As in the *Lectionary for Mass*, these selections correspond to the gospel. Nine sets of readings are provided for the weekdays of Lent.

THE SEASONS: ADVENT – CHRISTMAS

39. THE SEASON OF ADVENT. The first part of the Advent season extends from the First Sunday of Advent through December 16. The second part extends from December 17 through December 24.

40. The reign of God is already among us but is not yet made manifest in its fullness. As Christians, we celebrate what already is while standing in expectation of what is yet to be revealed. Though we cannot bring about the fullness of God's reign through our efforts alone we can cooperate with God's grace to be ready and vigilant for its advent (coming). The Advent season is one of vigilant waiting but not of Lenten penitence. The first part of the season of Advent directs the eyes of our faith to the fullness yet to be revealed when the Spirit-inspired vision of the prophets, especially Isaiah and John the Baptist, will become full reality. The second part prepares us to celebrate Christ's coming in the flesh at Bethlehem. This sense of vigilance and expectation should not be anticipated by civil, diocesan, parochial, or school celebrations of Christmas during the season of Advent.

41. The Sunday gospels in Advent treat the Lord's coming at the end of time (First Sunday of Advent), John the Baptist (Second and Third Sundays), and the events that immediately prepare for the Lord's birth (Fourth Sunday). The Old Testament readings, especially those from Isaiah, are prophecies about the Messiah and the Messianic age. The readings from the apostles serve as exhortations and as proclamations, in keeping with the different themes of Advent.[40] For the weekdays of Advent this Lectionary provides four sets of readings which reflect some of the major themes of the season.

42. THE SEASON OF CHRISTMAS. This season begins on the Vigil of Christmas and ends with the Feast of the Baptism of the Lord. The inauguration of the fullness we await was at long last disclosed in the incarnation and birth of Jesus (Christmas), born of Mary (Solemnity of Mary, Mother of God), who became a part of a human family (Feast of the Holy Family), was manifested to the nations (Epiphany), and revealed as God's own beloved child (Baptism of the Lord). The Christmas season celebrates the appearance of God among us in the birth, epiphany, and baptism of the Lord Jesus: the beginning of our salvation in Christ.

43. Christmas does not merely celebrate the birth of a child, rather this great feast celebrates the incarnation (birth) of the Lord of history in our world as God's own Word in our very flesh. It is the beginning of the paschal mystery and inevitably leads to his saving passion and resurrection from the dead. The full cycle of Christmas feasts, as surely as the celebration of the Easter Triduum, proclaims that God's "eternal Word has taken upon himself our human weakness."[41]

44. This is evident in the Gospel infancy narratives which, rather than being merely stories about the birth of a child, are anticipations of the acceptance and rejection which Jesus would meet throughout his ministry and unto his very death. Therefore Christmas is as integral to an adult understanding of faith as is Easter. Just as the Easter Triduum is one three-day celebration of Christ's paschal mystery, so the various feasts of the Christmas season are themselves celebrations of that same mystery made manifest in human history from the first moment of Jesus' birth. It is especially appropriate that the celebration of Christmas be prolonged throughout the Christmas season, rather than anticipating it as is so common in secular culture.

45. Only one set of readings for Christmas is provided in this Lectionary. These readings may be used for the Mass of the vigil, at midnight, at dawn, or during the day.

ORDINARY TIME
46. Ordinary Time comprises the thirty-three or thirty-four weeks of the liturgical year which follow the major seasons of Christmas and Easter. There are two periods of Ordinary Time: one which extends from the end of the Christmas season to the beginning of Lent; a longer one which extends from the end of the Easter season to the beginning of Advent. Ordinary Time is devoted to the mystery of Christ in all its aspects.[42] During these weeks the Gospel accounts of Jesus' ministry and teaching are proclaimed and celebrated. This Lectionary provides thirty-six sets of readings for use on the weekdays in Ordinary Time. All four gospels are represented in these weekday selections.

THE PROPER OF SAINTS
47. Throughout the centuries the Church has kept holy the memory of Mary, Mother of God, the apostles, the martyrs, and all the saints. The liturgy presents these men and women to us as intercessors and models. The entire Church joins in the celebrations of saints of universal significance, whereas other saints may be commemorated with optional celebrations by local churches or religious families.

48. Children's openness to the power of stories makes them ready listeners when they hear stories of the saints, the examples of whose lives give them a deeper appreciation of the gospel. This is especially true in the stories of saints of our time and nation. This Lectionary provides readings for all solemnities and for many feasts. Common readings are provided for use on other feasts and memorials.

IV. Particular Issues

PLACE OF CELEBRATION

49. The place where the liturgy of the word is celebrated may influence how the children receive God's word. It should be chosen carefully. Sometimes a space outside the usual place of worship may need to be chosen.[43] Even when classrooms or other non-liturgical spaces must be used for celebrations of the word with children every care must be taken that these spaces be well prepared, and that the environment is suitable for the worship of God.

THE LECTIONARY AND OTHER OBJECTS USED IN THE CELEBRATION

50. By their beauty and by the reverent way in which they are carried and handled the books used for the celebration of the word of God should be eloquent witnesses to the Church's reverence for the Scriptures.[44] The proclamation of the word transcends the mere communication of information and becomes a community-building celebration of God's saving mystery especially when candles, incense, banners, and processions magnify the word's impact on eyes and ears, in hearts and minds.

MUSIC

51. The eucharistic liturgy requires the full use of music which is integral to the whole celebration, including the proclamation of the word of God. The responsorial psalm is normally sung by a cantor with the assembly singing the refrain. The gospel acclamation must always be sung. A sung response to the petitions of the general intercessions can enhance participation.

PLAYS WITHIN THE LITURGY OF THE WORD

52. The Mass is not an historical reenactment of the events of salvation history and care should be taken not to give the impression that the liturgy of the word is a play. This is not to say that dramatic elements may not be used, e.g., the readings may at times be divided into parts distributed among the children;[45] however, the use of costumes, etc., is more appropriate in the context of other celebrations or services. Care should be taken especially at Christmas and during Holy Week and the Easter Triduum not to stage the various liturgies as plays. The Christmas Mass should not be presented as a birthday party for Jesus, nor should secular notions of Santa Claus be introduced into the Christmas liturgy.

COMMON FORMAT

53. The preparation and celebration of liturgies for children begin with and flow from a clear desire to assist them to participate in the worship of the entire community. This is best accomplished when the basic shape of the ritual used with the children, its symbols, gestures, and language, is similar

to that of the full assembly. The children are thus enabled to celebrate the paschal mystery of Christ on their own level of understanding and are led to the celebration of those same mysteries in the full assembly of the faithful.

Conclusion

54. Christ's particular care for children teaches us that they are capable of welcoming God's call and responding to it. Children's human and, therefore, religious experience is complete and whole in itself and is not determined simply by their potential for adulthood. The fullest reality of the liturgical assembly is children and adults together — not separate celebrations which run the risk of diminishing the place of children in the liturgical assembly. It should be noted that the same thing can happen if inadequate attention is given to their presence in the full assembly. Nevertheless, there will be occasions when a particular assembly is constituted almost entirely of children and other occasions where their numbers are so significant that the adaptations suggested by the Directory for Masses with Children should be applied for the sake of good pastoral care. This adaptation of the *Lectionary for Mass* is intended further to help those ministering to children. For them it provides the opportunity for deeper conversion as they attend to these young hearers of the word. The way in which the word of God is proclaimed and celebrated in the lives of children today will shape the future life of the Church.

Notes

[1] See John 1:1–3, 14.

[2] See Hebrews 1:1–3.

[3] Lectionary for Mass [=OLM], Introduction, no. 4.

[4] See Matthew 18:19–20; see also Constitution on the Liturgy, *Sacrosanctum Concilium* [=SC], art. 7.

[5] See SC, art. 7.

[6] See Directory for Masses with Children [=DMC], no. 8.

[7] See OLM, no. 6 and DMC, no. 15.

[8] See SC, art. 24, 35, and 56.

[9] See SC, art. 2; see also OLM, no. 10.

[10] OLM, no. 8.

[11] See DMC, nos. 22–24.

[12] DMC, no. 41.

[13] Ibid., no. 17.

[14] See DMC, nos. 20–21.

[15] DMC, no. 24.

[16] Ibid., no. 12.

17 See DMC, nos. 3 and 21.
18 See letter of the Congregation for Divine Worship and the Discipline of the Sacraments granting permission for the experimental use of the *Lectionary for Masses with Children* (Prot. N. 1259/91).
19 See DMC, no. 17.
20 See DMC, no. 16.
21 See DMC, no. 6.
22 DMC, no. 42.
23 See DMC, nos. 42–43.
24 See DMC, no. 43.
25 See DMC, no. 44.
26 See DMC, no. 30.
27 See DMC, no. 46.
28 See OLM, Introduction, no. 9.
29 See DMC, no. 12.
30 See DMC, nos. 33 and 34.
31 See DMC, no. 24.
32 See General Norms for the Liturgical Year and the Calendar [=GNLYC], no. 19.
33 Galatians 6:14.
34 Hebrews 10:12–14.
35 See GNLYC, no. 22.
36 Rite of Christian Initiation of Adults, no. 247.
37 See OLM, no. 100.
38 OLM, no. 100.
39 OLM, no. 97.
40 See OLM, no. 93.
41 *Roman Missal (Sacramentary)*, Preface of Christmas III.
42 GNLYC, no. 43.
43 See DMC, no. 25.
44 See OLM, no. 35.
45 See DMC, no. 47.

SEASON OF ADVENT

FIRST SUNDAY OF ADVENT

FIRST READING

Isaiah 2:1–5

The Lord will gather all nations in eternal peace in the kingdom of God.

A reading from the book of the prophet Isaiah

This is the vision that Isaiah son of Amoz had
  about Judah and Jerusalem:

In the future the mountain with the LORD's temple
    will be the highest of all.
It will reach above the hills,
and every nation will rush to it.
Many people will come and say,
"Let's go to the mountain of the LORD God of Jacob
    and worship in his temple."

The LORD will teach us his Law from Jerusalem.
He will settle the arguments of nations and of people.
They will pound their swords and their spears
    into garden tools.
And they will never make war or attack other nations.

People of Israel, let's live by the light of the LORD.

The word of the Lord.

Responsorial Psalm

*R. Let us go rejoicing
to the house of the Lord.*

*Psalm 122:1–2, 8–9
(see 1)*

*It made me glad to hear them say,
"Let's go to the house of the L*ORD*!"
Jerusalem, we are standing
inside your gates.*

*R. Let us go rejoicing
to the house of the Lord.*

*Because of my friends
and my relatives,
I will pray for peace.
And because of the house
of the L*ORD *our God,
I will work for your good.*

*R. Let us go rejoicing
to the house of the Lord.*

FIRST SUNDAY OF ADVENT

SECOND READING | **A reading from the letter of Paul to the Romans**

Romans 13:11–13a

Brothers and sisters:
You know what sort of times we live in,
and so you should live properly.
It is time to wake up.
You know that the day when we will be saved
   is nearer now than when we first put our faith in the Lord.
Night is almost over, and day will soon appear.
We must stop behaving as people do in the dark
and be ready to live in the light.
So behave properly, as people do in the day.

The time has come, our salvation is near.

The word of the Lord.

Alleluia   R. *Alleluia, Alleluia.*

Psalm 85:8

*Lord, show us your mercy and love,
and grant us your salvation.*

R. *Alleluia, Alleluia.*

GOSPEL

✠ A reading from the holy gospel according to Matthew

Matthew 24:37–44

Jesus said to his disciples:
"When the Son of Man appears,
things will be just as they were when Noah lived.
People were eating, drinking, and getting married
 right up to the day that the flood came
 and Noah went into the big boat.
They didn't know anything was happening
until the flood came and swept them all away.
That is how it will be when the Son of Man appears.

"Two men will be in the same field,
but only one will be taken.
The other will be left.
Two women will be together grinding grain,
but only one will be taken.
The other will be left.

"So be on your guard!
You don't know when your Lord will come.
Homeowners never know when a thief is coming,
and they are always on guard to keep one from breaking in.
Always be ready!
You don't know when the Son of Man will come."

The gospel of the Lord.

*Stay awake,
you must be ready.*

SECOND SUNDAY OF ADVENT

First Reading

Isaiah 11:1–4a, 5–6, 9b

He shall judge the poor with justice.

A reading from the book of the prophet Isaiah

The LORD says this:
Like a branch that sprouts from a stump,
someone from David's family will someday be king.
The Spirit of the LORD will take control of him
   and give him understanding and wisdom and insight.
He will be powerful,
and he will know and honor the LORD.
His greatest joy will be to worship the LORD.

He won't judge by appearances or listen to rumors.
The poor and the helpless will be treated
   with fairness and with justice.
Honesty and fairness will be his royal robes.

Leopards and young goats, and wolves and lambs
   will lie down and rest in the same field.
Calves and lions will eat together and be cared for by a child.

Just as water fills the sea,
the land will be filled with people
   who know and honor the LORD.

The word of the Lord.

Responsorial Psalm

R. *Justice shall flourish in his time,
and fullness of peace for ever.*

*Psalm 72:1 and 8, 17
(7)*

*Please help the king
to be honest and fair
just like you, our God.
Let his kingdom reach
from sea to sea,
from the Euphrates River
across all the earth.*

R. *Justice shall flourish in his time,
and fullness of peace for ever.*

*May the glory of the king
shine brightly forever
like the sun in the sky.
Let him make nations prosper
and learn to praise him.*

R. *Justice shall flourish in his time,
and fullness of peace for ever.*

SECOND READING

Romans 15:4–6

Christ, the hope of all people.

A reading from the letter of Paul to the Romans

Brothers and sisters:
The Scriptures were written to teach and encourage us
    by giving us hope.
God is the one who makes us patient and cheerful.
I pray that he will help you live at peace with each other,
as you follow Christ.
Then all of you together will praise God,
the Father of our Lord Jesus Christ.

The word of the Lord.

Alleluia

Luke 3:4, 6

R. Alleluia, Alleluia.

*Prepare the way of the Lord,
make straight his paths:
all people shall see
the salvation of God.*

R. Alleluia, Alleluia.

Gospel

Matthew 3:1–9, 11

✝ A reading from the holy gospel according to Matthew

John the Baptist started preaching in the desert of Judea.
He said, "Turn back to God!
The kingdom of heaven will soon be here."

John was the one the prophet Isaiah was talking about
    when he said,

   "In the desert someone is shouting,
   'Get the road ready for the Lord!
   Make a straight path for him.'"

John wore clothes made of camel's hair.
He had a leather strap around his waist
    and ate grasshoppers and wild honey.

From Jerusalem and all Judea
    and from the Jordan River Valley
    crowds of people went to John.
They told how sorry they were for their sins,
and he baptized them in the river.

Many Pharisees and Sadducees also came to be baptized.
But John said to them: "You bunch of snakes!
Who warned you to run from the coming judgment?
Do something to show
    that you have really given up your sins.
And don't start telling yourselves
    that you belong to Abraham's family.
I tell you that God can turn these stones
    into children for Abraham.

"I baptize you with water so that you will give up your sins.
But someone more powerful is going to come,
and I am not good enough even to carry his sandals.
He will baptize you with the Holy Spirit and with fire."

The gospel of the Lord.

Repent, for the kingdom of heaven is close at hand.

THIRD SUNDAY OF ADVENT

FIRST READING

A reading from the book of the prophet Isaiah

Isaiah 35:1–2, 5–6ab, 10

Thirsty deserts will be glad,
and barren lands will rejoice and blossom like flowers.
They will bloom everywhere and sing joyful songs.
They will be as majestic as Mount Lebanon
    and as glorious as Mount Carmel or the plain of Sharon.
Everyone will see the glory and the majesty
    of the LORD our God.

God will come and save you.

The blind will see, and the deaf will hear.
The disabled will leap about like deer,
and tongues once silent will shout.

The people the LORD has rescued will come back singing,
as they enter Zion.
Happiness will be a crown they will always wear.
They will rejoice and be glad,
because all sorrows and worries will be gone.

The word of the Lord.

Responsorial Psalm

R. Lord, come and save us.

God always keeps his word.
He gives justice to the poor
and food to the hungry.

Psalm 146:6d–7ab, 7c–8abc, 10
(Isaiah 35:4)

R. Lord, come and save us.

The LORD sets prisoners free
and heals blind eyes.
He gives a helping hand
to everyone who falls.

R. Lord, come and save us.

The LORD God of Zion
will rule forever!
Shout praises to the LORD!

R. Lord, come and save us.

Second Reading

James 5:7–10

You also must be patient; do not lose heart, the Lord's coming will be soon.

A reading from the letter of James

My friends, be patient until the Lord returns.
Think of farmers who wait patiently
   for the spring and summer rains
   to make their valuable crops grow.
Be patient like those farmers and don't give up.
The Lord will soon be here!
Don't grumble about each other or you will be judged,
and the judge is right outside the door.

My friends, follow the example of the prophets
   who spoke for the Lord.
They were patient,
even when they had to suffer.

The word of the Lord.

Alleluia

Isaiah 61:1

R. *Alleluia, Alleluia.*

*The Spirit of the Lord now upon me
has sent me to bring good news
to the poor.*

R. *Alleluia, Alleluia.*

THIRD SUNDAY OF ADVENT

✢ A reading from the holy gospel according to Matthew

GOSPEL

Matthew 11:2–11

John was in prison when he heard what Christ was doing.
So John sent some of his followers to ask Jesus,
"Are you the one we should be looking for?
Or must we wait for someone else?"

Jesus answered,
   "Go and tell John what you have heard and seen.
The blind are now able to see,
and the lame can walk.
People with leprosy are being healed,
and the deaf can hear.
The dead are raised to life,
and the poor are hearing the good news.
God will bless everyone who does not reject me
   because of what I do."

As John's followers were going away,
Jesus spoke to the crowds about John:
"What sort of person did you go out into the desert to see?
Was he like tall grass blown about by the wind?

"What kind of man did you go out to see?
Was he someone dressed in fine clothes?
People who dress like that live in the king's palace.

"What did you really go out to see?
Was he a prophet? He certainly was.
I tell you that he was more than a prophet.
In the Scriptures God says about him,

   'I am sending my messenger ahead of you
   to get things ready for you.'

"I tell you that no one ever born on this earth
   is greater than John the Baptist.
But whoever is least in the kingdom of heaven
   is greater than John."

The gospel of the Lord.

Are you the one who is to come, or must we wait for someone else?

FOURTH SUNDAY OF ADVENT

First Reading

Romans 1:2–4

Jesus Christ, a descendant of David, is the Son of God.

A reading from the letter of Paul to the Romans

Brothers and sisters:
Long ago God promised the good news
   by what his prophets said in the holy Scriptures.
This good news is about his Son, our Lord Jesus Christ!
As a human, he was from the family of David.
But the Holy Spirit proved that Jesus
   is the powerful Son of God,
because he was raised from death.

The word of the Lord.

Responsorial Psalm R. *Let the Lord enter; he is king of glory.*

The earth and everything on it
belong to the LORD.
The world and its people
belong to him.
The LORD placed it all
on the oceans and rivers.

Psalm 24:1–2, 3–4abc
(7c and 10b)

R. *Let the Lord enter; he is king of glory.*

Who may climb the LORD's hill
or stand in his holy temple?
Only those who do right
for the right reasons,
and don't worship idols.

R. *Let the Lord enter; he is king of glory.*

Alleluia

R. *Alleluia, Alleluia.*

Matthew 1:23

A virgin will give birth to a son;
his name will be Emmanuel:
God is with us.

R. *Alleluia, Alleluia.*

GOSPEL

✢ **A reading from the holy gospel according to Matthew**

Matthew 1:18–24

This is how Jesus Christ was born.
A young woman named Mary was engaged to Joseph
   from King David's family.
But before they were married,
she learned that she was going to have a baby
   by God's Holy Spirit.

Jesus was born of Mary,
the betrothed of Joseph,
a son of David.

Joseph was a good man and did not want to embarrass Mary
   in front of everyone.
So he decided to quietly call off the wedding.

While Joseph was thinking about this,
an angel from the Lord came to him in a dream.
The angel said, "Joseph, the baby that Mary will have
    is from the Holy Spirit.
Go ahead and marry her.
Then after her baby is born, name him Jesus,
because he will save his people from their sins."

So God's promise came true, just as the prophet had said,

> "A virgin will have a baby boy,
> and he will be called Immanuel,"
> which means "God is with us."

After Joseph woke up, he and Mary were soon married,
just as the Lord's angel had told him to do.

The gospel of the Lord.

Season of Christmas

THE BIRTH OF THE LORD

December 25

The following readings may be used only when the celebration of the liturgy of the word for the children is held in a place apart from the main assembly.

FIRST READING

Isaiah 9:2–4, 6–7

A son is given to us.

A reading from the book of the prophet Isaiah

Those who walked in the dark have seen a bright light.
And it shines upon everyone who lives
   in the land of darkest shadows.

Our LORD, you have made your nation stronger.
Because of you, its people are glad and celebrate
   like workers at harvest time
   or soldiers dividing what they have taken.

You have broken the power
   of those who oppressed and enslaved your people.
You have rescued them as you did from Midian.

For us a child has been born.
A son has been given to us,
and he will be our ruler.
His names will be:
Wonderful Adviser and Mighty God,
Eternal Father and Prince of Peace.

His power will never end,
and peace will last forever.
He will rule David's kingdom and make it grow strong.
He will always rule with honesty and justice.
The LORD All-Powerful will make certain
   that all of this is done.

The word of the Lord.

Responsorial Psalm

R. *Today is born our Savior, Christ the Lord.*

Sing a new song to the LORD*!*
Everyone on this earth,
sing praises to the LORD*,*
sing and praise his name.

Psalm 96:1–2a, 2b–3, 11–12a
(Luke 2:11)

R. *Today is born our Savior, Christ the Lord.*

Day after day announce,
"The LORD *has saved us!"*
Tell every nation on earth,
"The LORD *is wonderful*
and does marvelous things!"

R. *Today is born our Savior, Christ the Lord.*

Tell the heavens and the earth
to be glad and celebrate!
Command the ocean to roar
with all of its creatures
and the fields to rejoice
with all of their crops.

R. *Today is born our Savior, Christ the Lord.*

Second Reading

Titus 3:4–6

God's grace has been revealed to all people.

A reading from the letter of Paul to Titus

Brothers and sisters:
God our Savior showed us how good and kind he is.
He saved us because of his mercy,
and not because of any good things that we have done.

God washed us by the power of the Holy Spirit.
He gave us new birth and a fresh beginning.
God sent Jesus Christ our Savior to give us his Spirit.

The word of the Lord.

Alleluia

Luke 2:10–11

R. Alleluia, alleluia.

*Good news and great joy
to all the world:
today is born our Savior,
Christ the Lord.*

R. Alleluia, alleluia.

GOSPEL

Luke 2:1–14

✠ A reading from the holy gospel according to Luke

Emperor Augustus gave orders
  for the names of all the people
  to be listed in record books.
These first records were made
  when Quirinius was governor of Syria.

Everyone had to go to their own hometown to be listed.
So Joseph had to leave Nazareth in Galilee
  and go to Bethlehem in Judea.
Long ago Bethlehem had been King David's hometown,
and Joseph went there because he was from David's family.

Mary was engaged to Joseph
  and traveled with him to Bethlehem.
She was soon going to have a baby,
and while they were there,
she gave birth to her first-born son.
She dressed him in baby clothes and laid him in a manger,
because there was no room for them in the inn.

That night in the fields near Bethlehem
  some shepherds were guarding their sheep.
All at once an angel came down to them from the Lord,
and the brightness of the Lord's glory flashed around them.
The shepherds were frightened.
But the angel said, "Don't be afraid!
I have good news for you, which will make everyone happy.
This very day in King David's hometown
  a Savior was born for you.
He is Christ the Lord.
You will know who he is,
because you will find him dressed in baby clothes
  and lying in a manger."

Suddenly many other angels came down from heaven
  and joined in praising God.
They said: "Praise God in heaven!
Peace on earth to everyone who pleases God."

The gospel of the Lord.

Today a Savior has been born for you.

THE HOLY FAMILY
Sunday in the Octave of Christmas

FIRST READING

A reading from the book of Sirach

Sirach 3:2–6

Children, the LORD expects you to honor your father,
and has given your mother authority over you.

If you honor your father,
your sins will be forgiven.
If you praise your mother,
treasure will be stored up in heaven for you.

Those who fear the Lord honor their parents.

If you honor your father,
your own children will make you happy,
and all of your prayers will be answered.
If you respect your father,
you will live a long life,
and if you listen to the LORD,
your mother can relax.

The word of the Lord.

Responsorial Psalm

R. *Happy are those who fear the Lord and walk in his ways.*

Psalm 128:1–2, 3, 4–5
(see 1)

*The LORD will bless you
if you respect him
and obey his laws.
Your fields will produce,
and you will be happy
and all will go well.*

R. *Happy are those who fear the Lord and walk in his ways.*

*Your wife will be as fruitful
as a grapevine,
and just as an olive tree
is rich with olives,
your home will be rich
with healthy children.*

R. *Happy are those who fear the Lord and walk in his ways.*

*That is how the LORD will bless
everyone who respects him.
I pray that the LORD
will bless you from Zion
and let Jerusalem prosper
as long as you live.*

R. *Happy are those who fear the Lord and walk in his ways.*

SECOND READING

Colossians 3:12–17

Concerning the Christian life in the world.

A reading from the letter of Paul to the Colossians

Brothers and sisters:
God loves you and has chosen you as his own special people.
So be gentle, kind, humble, meek, and patient.
Put up with each other,
and forgive anyone who does you wrong,
  just as Christ has forgiven you.
Love is more important than anything else.
It is what ties everything completely together.

Each one of you is part of the body of Christ,
and you were chosen to live together in peace.
So let the peace that comes from Christ
   control your thoughts.
And be grateful.

Let the message about Christ completely fill your lives,
while you use all your wisdom
   to teach and instruct each other.
With thankful hearts,
   sing psalms, hymns, and spiritual songs to God.
Whatever you say or do should be done
   in the name of the Lord Jesus,
as you give thanks to God the Father because of him.

The word of the Lord.

Alleluia

Colossians 3:15a, 16

R. *Alleluia, alleluia.*

May the peace of Christ
rule in your hearts,
and the fullness of his message
live within you.

R. *Alleluia, alleluia.*

GOSPEL

Matthew 2:13–15, 19–23

✚ **A reading from the holy gospel according to Matthew**

An angel from the Lord appeared to Joseph in a dream.
The angel said, "Get up!
Hurry and take the child and his mother to Egypt!
Stay there until I tell you to return,
because Herod is looking for the child
  and wants to kill him."

That night Joseph got up
  and took his wife and the child to Egypt,
where they stayed until Herod died.
So the Lord's promise came true,
  just as the prophet had said,
"I called my son out of Egypt."

After King Herod died,
an angel from the Lord appeared in a dream to Joseph
while he was still in Egypt.
The angel said, "Get up and take the child and his mother
  back to Israel.
The people who wanted to kill him are now dead."

Joseph got up and left with them for Israel.
But when he heard
  that Herod's son Archelaus was now ruler of Judea,
he was afraid to go there.
Then in a dream he was told to go to Galilee,
and they went to live there in the town of Nazareth.

So the Lord's promise came true,
just as the prophet had said,
"He will be called a Nazarene."

The gospel of the Lord.

Take the child and his mother, and flee to Egypt.

MARY, MOTHER OF GOD
January 1, Octave of Christmas

FIRST READING

Numbers 6:22–27

They will call down my name on the children of Israel, and I will bless them.

A reading from the book of Numbers

The LORD told Moses to tell Aaron and his sons
what they must say to bless the people of Israel.
It was:
"I pray that the LORD will bless and protect you.
May the LORD show kindness and mercy to you.
May he be good to you and give you peace."

Then the LORD said,
"If they speak in my name to the people of Israel,
I will bless them."

The word of the Lord.

Responsorial Psalm R. *May God bless us in his mercy.*

Our God, be kind and bless us!
Be pleased and smile.
Then everyone on earth
will learn to follow you,
and all nations will see
your power to save us.

Psalm 67:1–2, 5 and 7
(2a)

R. *May God bless us in his mercy.*

Make everyone praise you
and shout your praises.
Pray for his blessings to continue
and for everyone on earth
to worship our God.

R. *May God bless us in his mercy.*

Alleluia

R. Alleluia, alleluia.

Hebrews 1:1–2

In the past God spoke to our ancestors
through the prophets;
now God speaks to us
through the Son.

R. Alleluia, alleluia.

GOSPEL

✠ **A reading from the holy gospel according to Luke**

Luke 2:16–21

The shepherds hurried off and found Mary and Joseph,
and they saw the baby lying in the manger.

When the shepherds saw Jesus,
they told his parents what the angel had said about him.
Everyone listened and was surprised.
But Mary kept thinking about all this
   and wondering what it meant.

The shepherds found Mary and Joseph, and the baby lying in the manger.... When the eighth day came they gave him the name Jesus.

As the shepherds returned to their sheep,
they were praising God
   and saying wonderful things about him.
Everything they had seen and heard
   was just as the angel had said.

Eight days later Jesus' parents did for him
   what the Law of Moses commands.
And they named him Jesus,
just as the angel had told Mary
   when he promised she would have a baby.

The gospel of the Lord.

THE EPIPHANY OF THE LORD

The following readings may be used only when the celebration of the liturgy of the word for the children is held in a place apart from the main assembly.

First Reading | **A reading from the book of the prophet Isaiah**

Isaiah 60:1–6

The glory of the Lord shines upon you.

Jerusalem, stand up and shine!
Your new day is dawning.
And the glory of the Lord shines brightly on you.
The earth and its people are covered with darkness,
but the glory of the Lord is shining over you.
Nations and kings will come to the light
    of your dawning day.

Open your eyes and look around!
Crowds are on their way.
Your sons are coming from distant lands,
and your daughters are being carried like young children.
When you see this, your faces will glow.
Your hearts will beat fast and swell with pride.

Treasures from over the sea
and the wealth of nations will be brought to you.
Your country will be covered with caravans of young camels
    from Midian and Ephah.
And the people of Sheba will bring gold and spices
    in praise of the Lord.

The word of the Lord.

Responsorial Psalm

*R. Lord, every nation on earth
will adore you.*

*Please help the king
to be honest and fair
just like you, our God.*

Psalm 72:1, 2, 10abc, 10de–11
(see 11)

*R. Lord, every nation on earth
will adore you.*

*Let him be honest and fair
with all your people,
especially the poor.*

*R. Lord, every nation on earth
will adore you.*

*Force the rulers of Tarshish
and of the islands
to pay taxes to him.*

*R. Lord, every nation on earth
will adore you.*

*Make the kings of Sheba
and of Seba bring gifts.
Make other rulers bow down
and all nations serve him.*

*R. Lord, every nation on earth
will adore you.*

Alleluia

R. Alleluia, alleluia.

Matthew 2:2

We have seen his star in the east
and have come to adore the Lord.

R. Alleluia, alleluia.

GOSPEL

✠ A reading from the holy gospel according to Matthew

Matthew 2:1–12

When Jesus was born in the village of Bethlehem in Judea,
Herod was king.
During this time some wise men from the east
   came to Jerusalem and said,
"Where is the child born to be king of the Jews?
We saw his star in the east and have come to worship him."

We have come from the east to worship the king.

When King Herod heard about this, he was worried,
and so was everyone else in Jerusalem.
Herod brought together all the chief priests and the teachers
   of the Law of Moses and asked them,
"Where will the Messiah be born?"

They told him,
"He will be born in Bethlehem, just as the prophet wrote,

   'Bethlehem in the land of Judea,
   you are very important among the towns of Judea.
   From your town will come a leader,
   who will be like a shepherd for my people Israel.'"

Herod secretly called in the wise men
   and asked them when they had first seen the star.
He told them, "Go to Bethlehem
   and search carefully for the child.
As soon as you find him, let me know.
I want to go and worship him too."

The wise men listened to what the king said and then left.
And the star they had seen in the east
   went on ahead of them
until it stopped over the place where the child was.
They were thrilled and excited to see the star.

When the men went into the house
   and saw the child with Mary, his mother,
they kneeled down and worshiped him.
They took out their gifts of gold, frankincense, and myrrh
   and gave them to him.
Later they were warned in a dream not to return to Herod,
and they went back home by another road.

The gospel of the Lord.

THE BAPTISM OF THE LORD

Sunday after January 6
First Sunday in Ordinary Time

FIRST READING

Isaiah 42:1–2, 4, 6–7

Here is my servant, my chosen one in whom I am well pleased.

A reading from the book of the prophet Isaiah

Here is my servant!
I have made him strong.
He is my chosen one, and I am pleased with him.

I will give him my Spirit,
and he will bring justice to the nations.
He won't shout or yell or call out in the streets.
He won't quit or give up
   until he brings justice to all the earth,
and people in foreign lands long for his teaching.

I, the LORD, chose you because of my kindness,
and I am here at your side.
I created and appointed you
   to bring light and my promise of hope to the nations.
You will give sight to the blind
   and set prisoners free from dark dungeons.

The word of the Lord.

Responsorial Psalm

Psalm 29:3abde–4, 3cde and 9ef–10 (11b)

R. The Lord will bless his people with peace.

The voice of the LORD echoes over the oceans. He thunders above the roar of the raging seas, and his voice is mighty and marvelous.

R. The Lord will bless his people with peace.

The glorious LORD God thunders above the roar of the raging seas, and the temple is filled with shouts of praise. The LORD rules on his throne, king of the flood forever.

R. The Lord will bless his people with peace.

THE BAPTISM OF THE LORD

SECOND READING

Acts 10:34–38

God anointed Jesus of Nazareth with the Holy Spirit and with power.

A reading from the Acts of the Apostles

Peter said to Cornelius and his household:
"Now I am certain that God treats all people alike.
God is pleased with everyone who worships him
    and does right,
no matter what nation they come from.
This is the same message
    that God gave to the people of Israel,
when he sent Jesus Christ, the Lord of all,
    to offer peace to them.

"You surely know what happened everywhere in Judea.
It all began in Galilee
    after John had told everyone to be baptized.
God gave the Holy Spirit and power
    to Jesus from Nazareth.
He was with Jesus,
as he went around doing good
    and healing everyone
    who was under the power of the devil."

The word of the Lord.

Alleluia

See Mark 9:7

R. *Alleluia, alleluia.*

*The heavens were opened
and the Father's voice was heard:
This is my beloved Son, hear him.*

R. *Alleluia, alleluia.*

GOSPEL

Luke 3:15–16, 21–22

✚ **A reading from the holy gospel according to Luke**

Everyone became excited and wondered,
"Could John be the Messiah?"

John said, "I am just baptizing with water.
But someone more powerful is going to come,
and I am not good enough even to untie his sandals.
He will baptize you with the Holy Spirit and with fire."

After everyone else had been baptized,
Jesus himself was baptized.
Then as he prayed, the sky opened up,
and the Holy Spirit came down upon him
   in the form of a dove.
A voice from heaven said,
"You are my own dear Son, and I am pleased with you."

The gospel of the Lord.

When Jesus had been baptized and had been praying, the heavens were opened and the Holy Spirit came upon him.

SEASON OF LENT

FIRST SUNDAY OF LENT

The following readings may be used only when the celebration of the liturgy of the word for the children is held in a place apart from the main assembly.

First Reading | **A reading from the book of Genesis**

Genesis 2:7–9; 3:1–7

The Lord God took some earth
and used it to make a man.
God breathed into the man's nose,
and the man started breathing.
The Lord God had made a garden in a place called Eden,
which was in the east,
and he put the man there.

Creation of our first parents, and sin.

The Lord made all kinds of beautiful trees
and all kinds of fruit trees grow in the garden.
Two other trees were in the middle of the garden.
One of the trees gave life,
and the other showed the difference
between right and wrong.

The snake was sneakier than any of the other wild animals
that the Lord God had made.
One day it came to the woman and asked,
"Did God tell you not to eat fruit
from any tree in the garden?"

The woman answered,
"God said we could eat fruit from any tree in the garden
except the one in the middle.
He told us not to eat fruit from that tree or even touch it.
If we do, we will die."

"No, you won't die!" the snake replied.
"God understands what will happen
on the day you eat fruit from that tree.
You will see what you have done,
and you will know the difference between right and wrong,
just as God does."

The woman stared at the fruit.
It looked beautiful and tasty.
She wanted the wisdom that it would give her,
and she ate some of the fruit.
She gave some to her husband Adam, and he ate it too.
At once they saw what they had done,
and they realized that they were naked.
So they sewed fig leaves together
   to make clothes for themselves.

The word of the Lord.

Responsorial Psalm

*R. Be merciful, O Lord,
for we have sinned.*

*You are kind, God!
Please have pity on me.
You are always merciful!
Please wipe away my sins.*

Psalm 51:1, 10, 12, 15
(3a)

*R. Be merciful, O Lord,
for we have sinned.*

*Create pure thoughts in me
and make me faithful again.*

*R. Be merciful, O Lord,
for we have sinned.*

*Make me as happy as you did
when you saved me;
make me want to obey!*

continued

R. Be merciful, O Lord,
for we have sinned.

Help me to speak,
and I will praise you, Lord.

R. Be merciful, O Lord,
for we have sinned.

Verse before the Gospel

Matthew 4:4b

R. Glory and praise to you,
Lord Jesus Christ.

No one lives on bread alone,
but on every word that comes
from the mouth of God.

R. Glory and praise to you,
Lord Jesus Christ.

GOSPEL

Matthew 4:1–11

Jesus fasted for forty days and nights and was tempted.

✚ **A reading from the holy gospel according to Matthew**

The Holy Spirit led Jesus into the desert,
so that the devil could test him.
After Jesus went without eating for forty days and nights,
he was very hungry.
Then the devil came to him and said,
"If you are God's Son,
tell these stones to turn into bread."

Jesus answered,
"The Scriptures say: 'No one can live only on food.
People need every word that God has spoken.'"

Next, the devil took Jesus to the holy city
   and had him stand on the highest part of the temple.

The devil said, "If you are God's Son, jump off.
The Scriptures say:
   'God will give his angels orders about you.
They will catch you in their arms,
and you will not hurt your feet on the stones.'"

Jesus answered, "The Scriptures also say,
'Don't try to test the Lord your God!'"

Finally, the devil took Jesus up on a very high mountain
   and showed him all the kingdoms on earth
   and their power.
The devil said to him, "I will give all this to you,
if you will bow down and worship me."

Jesus answered, "Go away, Satan!
The Scriptures say:
   'Worship the Lord your God and serve only him.'"

Then the devil left Jesus,
and angels came to help him.

The gospel of the Lord.

SECOND SUNDAY OF LENT

The following readings may be used only when the celebration of the liturgy of the word for the children is held in a place apart from the main assembly.

FIRST READING

A reading from the book of Genesis

Genesis 12:1–4a

The LORD said to Abraham,
"Leave your country, your family, and your relatives
and go to the land that I will show you.

"I will bless you and make you into a great nation.
You will become famous and be a blessing to others.
I will bless the people who say good things about you,
but I will put a curse on anyone
    who says evil things about you.
Everyone on earth will be blessed because of you."
So Abraham left, just as the LORD had told him to do.

The word of the Lord.

The call of Abraham, the father of God's people.

Responsorial Psalm

R. Lord, let your mercy be on us,
as we place our trust in you.

Psalm 33:4–5, 20 and 22
(22)

The LORD is truthful;
he can be trusted.
He loves justice and fairness,
and he is kind to everyone
everywhere on earth.

R. Lord, let your mercy be on us,
as we place our trust in you.

We depend on you, LORD,
to help and protect us.
Be kind and bless us!
We depend on you.

R. Lord, let your mercy be on us,
as we place our trust in you.

Verse before the Gospel

See Matthew 17:5

*R. Glory and praise to you,
Lord Jesus Christ.*

*From the shining cloud
the Father's voice is heard:
This is my beloved Son, hear him.*

*R. Glory and praise to you,
Lord Jesus Christ.*

GOSPEL

Matthew 17:1–9

Jesus' face shone like the sun.

✠ **A reading from the holy gospel according to Matthew**

Jesus took Peter and the brothers James and John with him.
They went up on a very high mountain
   where they could be alone.
There in front of the disciples Jesus was completely changed.
His face was shining like the sun,
and his clothes became white as light.

All at once Moses and Elijah were there talking with Jesus.
So Peter said to him, "Lord, it is good for us to be here!
Let us make three shelters,
one for you, one for Moses, and one for Elijah."

While Peter was still speaking,
the shadow of a bright cloud passed over them.
From the cloud a voice said,
"This is my own dear Son, and I am pleased with him.
Listen to what he says!"

When the disciples heard the voice,
they were so afraid that they fell flat on the ground.
But Jesus came over and touched them.
He said, "Get up and don't be afraid!"
When they opened their eyes, they saw only Jesus.

On their way down from the mountain,
Jesus warned his disciples not to tell anyone
    what they had seen
until after the Son of Man had been raised from death.

The gospel of the Lord.

THIRD SUNDAY OF LENT

The following readings may be used only when the celebration of the liturgy of the word for the children is held in a place apart from the main assembly.

FIRST READING | **A reading from the book of Exodus**

Exodus 17:3–7

The people of Israel were thirsty and kept on complaining.
They said, "Moses, did you bring us out of Egypt
just to let us and our families and our animals die of thirst?"

Then Moses prayed,
   "LORD, what am I going to do with these people?
They are about to stone me to death."

Give us water to drink (Exodus 17:2).

The LORD answered, "Take some of the leaders with you
and go on ahead of the rest of the people.
Take along the walking stick
   that you used to strike the Nile River,
and when you get to the rock at Sinai,
I will be there with you.
Strike the rock with the stick,
and water will pour out for the people to drink."

Moses did this while the leaders of the people watched.
He named that place Massah and Meribah.
This was because the people complained
   and tested the LORD by asking,
"Is the LORD really with us?"

The word of the Lord.

Responsorial Psalm R. *If today you hear God's voice,*
harden not your hearts.

*Sing joyful songs to the L*ORD*!*
Praise the mighty rock
Psalm 95:1–2, 7e–9c *where we are safe.*
(8) *Come to worship him*
with thankful hearts
and songs of praise.

R. *If today you hear God's voice,*
harden not your hearts.

Listen to God's voice today!
Don't be stubborn and rebel
as your ancestors did
at Meribah and at Massah
out in the desert.
They tested God and saw
the things he did.

R. *If today you hear God's voice,*
harden not your hearts.

Verse before the Gospel

See John 2:42, 15

R. Glory and praise to you,
Lord Jesus Christ.

Lord, you are truly
the Savior of the world;
give me living water,
that I may never thirst again.

R. Glory and praise to you,
Lord Jesus Christ.

GOSPEL

John 4:5–15, 19b–26,
39a, 40–42

The water that I shall give will become a spring of eternal life.

✚ **A reading from the holy gospel according to John**

On his way to Galilee,
Jesus came to the town of Sychar.
It was near the field that Jacob had long ago given
    to his son Joseph.
The well that Jacob had dug was still there,
and Jesus sat down beside it
because he was tired from traveling.
It was noon,
and after Jesus' disciples had gone into town
    to buy some food,
a Samaritan woman came to draw water from the well.

Jesus asked her,
    "Would you please give me a drink of water?"

"You are a Jew," she replied,
"and I am a Samaritan woman.
How can you ask me for a drink of water
when Jews and Samaritans won't have anything to do
    with each other?"

Jesus answered,
   "You don't know what God wants to give you,
and you don't know who is asking you for a drink.
If you did, you would ask him for the water that gives life."

"Sir," the woman said,
"you don't even have a bucket, and the well is deep.
Where are you going to get this life-giving water?
Our ancestor Jacob dug this well for us,
and his family and animals got water from it.
Are you greater than Jacob?"

Jesus answered,
"Everyone who drinks this water will get thirsty again.
But no one who drinks the water I give
   will ever be thirsty again.
The water I give is like a flowing fountain
   that gives eternal life."

The woman replied,
   "Sir, please give me a drink of that water!
Then I won't get thirsty
   and have to come to this well again."

She also told him,
"Sir, I can see that you are a prophet.
My ancestors worshiped on this mountain,
but you Jews say Jerusalem is the only place to worship."

continued

Jesus said to her: "Believe me,
the time is coming when you won't worship God
   either on this mountain or in Jerusalem.
You Samaritans don't really know the one you worship.
But we Jews do know the God we worship,
and by using us God will save the world.
But a time is coming, and it is already here!
Even now the true worshipers are being led by the Spirit
   to worship the Father according to the truth.
These are the ones the Father is seeking to worship him.
God is Spirit,
and those who worship God must be led by the Spirit
   to worship him according to the truth."

The woman said, "I know that the Messiah will come.
He is the one we call Christ.
When he comes, he will explain everything to us."

"I am that one," Jesus told her,
"and I am speaking to you now."

A lot of Samaritans in that town put their faith in Jesus.
They came and asked him to stay in their town,
and he stayed on for two days.

Many more Samaritans put their faith in Jesus
because of what they heard him say.
They told the woman, "We no longer have faith in Jesus
   just because of what you told us.
We have heard him ourselves,
and we are certain that he is the Savior of the world!"

The gospel of the Lord.

THIRD SUNDAY OF LENT

FOURTH SUNDAY OF LENT

The following readings may be used only when the celebration of the liturgy of the word for the children is held in a place apart from the main assembly.

FIRST READING

A reading from the first book of Samuel

1 Samuel 16:1b, 6–7, 10–13a

The LORD said to Samuel:
"Take some olive oil with you
and go to a man named Jesse who lives in Bethlehem.
I have chosen one of his sons to be king."

David is anointed king of Israel.

When Jesse and his sons got there,
Samuel saw Jesse's oldest son, Eliab, and thought,
"He must be the one the LORD has chosen."

But the LORD told Samuel,
"Don't choose him just because he is tall and handsome.
He isn't the one I have chosen.
People judge others by what they look like, but I don't.
I judge by what is in a person's heart."

Jesse sent seven of his sons to Samuel,
but each time Samuel would say,
"The LORD has not chosen him."

Finally, Samuel asked Jesse,
"Do you have any more sons?"

Jesse answered,
"Yes, my youngest son David
   is out taking care of the sheep."

Samuel said, "Send for him.
We won't start until he gets here."

Jesse sent for David, and he came.
He was a healthy, good-looking boy
   with a sparkle in his eyes.
The LORD told Samuel, "This is the one.
Pour the olive oil on his head."
Samuel poured the oil on David's head
   while his brothers watched.
At that moment the LORD's Spirit took control of David
   and stayed with him from then on.

The word of the Lord.

Responsorial Psalm

Psalm 23:1–3a, 3b–4, 5b–6c
(1)

R. *The Lord is my shepherd;
there is nothing I shall want.*

*You, LORD, are my shepherd.
I will never be in need.
You let me rest in fields
of green grass.
You lead me to streams
of peaceful water,
and you refresh my life.*

R. *The Lord is my shepherd;
there is nothing I shall want.*

*You are true to your name,
and you lead me
along the right paths.
I may walk through valleys
as dark as death,
but I won't be afraid.
You are with me,
and your shepherd's rod
makes me feel safe.*

R. *The Lord is my shepherd;
there is nothing I shall want.*

*While my enemies watch,
you honor me as your guest,
and you fill my cup
until it overflows.
Your kindness and love
will always be with me
each day of my life.*

R. *The Lord is my shepherd;
there is nothing I shall want.*

SECOND READING

Ephesians 5:1-2, 8-10

A reading from the letter of Paul to the Ephesians

Brothers and sisters:
Do as God does.
After all, you are his dear children.
Let love be your guide.
Christ loved us and offered his life for us
   as a sacrifice that pleases God.

You used to be like people living in the dark,
but now you are people of the light
because you belong to the Lord.
So act like people of the light
and make your light shine.
Be good and honest and truthful,
as you try to please the Lord.

The word of the Lord.

You are people of the light.

Verse before the Gospel

John 8:12

*R. Glory and praise to you,
Lord Jesus Christ.*

*I am the light of the world,
says the Lord;
whoever follows me
will have the light of life.*

*R. Glory and praise to you,
Lord Jesus Christ.*

GOSPEL

John 9:1, 6–12, 35–38

The man who was blind went off and washed himself and came away with his sight restored.

✠ **A reading from the holy gospel according to John**

One day as Jesus walked along,
he saw a man who had been blind since birth.
Jesus spit on the ground.
He made some mud and smeared it on the man's eyes.
Then he said, "Go and wash off the mud in Siloam Pool."
The man went and washed in Siloam,
which means "One Who Is Sent."
When he had washed off the mud, he could see.

The man's neighbors
  and the people who had seen him begging
    wondered if he really could be the same man.
Some of them said he was the same beggar,
while others said he only looked like him.
But he told them, "I am that man."

"Then how can you see?" they asked.

He answered,
"Someone named Jesus made some mud
  and smeared it on my eyes.
He told me to go and wash it off in Siloam Pool.
When I did, I could see."

"Where is he now?" they asked.
"I don't know," he answered.

When Jesus heard what had happened,
he went and found the man.

Then Jesus asked, "Do you have faith in the Son of Man?"
He replied, "Sir, if you will tell me who he is,
I will put my faith in him."

"You have already seen him," Jesus answered,
"and right now he is talking with you."
The man said, "Lord, I put my faith in you!"
Then he worshiped Jesus.

The gospel of the Lord.

FIFTH SUNDAY OF LENT

The following readings may be used only when the celebration of the liturgy of the word for the children is held in a place apart from the main assembly.

FIRST READING

A reading from the book of the prophet Ezekiel

Ezekiel 37:12–14

I shall put my spirit in you, and you will live.

The LORD said to Ezekiel:
Tell the people that I, the LORD God,
   promise to open their graves and set them free,
so they can go home to their land.
When I let them out of their graves,
they will know that I am the LORD.
My Spirit will give them breath.
They will live again,
and I will bring them back home.
Then they will know that I, the LORD God,
have kept my promise.

The word of the Lord.

Responsorial Psalm

Psalm 130:1–2, 5 and 7bcd (7bc)

*R. With the Lord there is mercy
and fullness of redemption.*

*From a sea of troubles
I call out to you, LORD.
Won't you please listen
as I beg for mercy?*

*R. With the Lord there is mercy
and fullness of redemption.*

*With all my heart,
I am waiting, LORD, for you!
I trust your promises.
God is always merciful,
and he has the power to save you.*

*R. With the Lord there is mercy
and fullness of redemption.*

Verse before the Gospel

John 11:25, 26

R. *Glory and praise to you,
Lord Jesus Christ.*

*I am the resurrection and the life,
says the Lord;
whoever believes in me
will not die for ever.*

R. *Glory and praise to you,
Lord Jesus Christ.*

GOSPEL

John 11:3–7, 17, 20–27,
31–45

*I am the resurrection
and the life.*

✠ **A reading from the holy gospel according to John**

Martha and her sister Mary sent a message to the Lord
and told him that his good friend Lazarus was sick.

When Jesus heard this, he said,
"His sickness won't end in death.
It will bring glory to God and his Son."

Jesus loved Martha and her sister and brother.
But he stayed where he was for two more days.
Then he said to his disciples,
"Now we'll go back to Judea."

When Jesus got to Bethany,
he found that Lazarus
    had already been in the tomb four days.

When Martha heard that Jesus had arrived,
she went out to meet him,
but Mary stayed in the house.
Martha said to Jesus, "Lord, if you had been here,
my brother would not have died.
Yet even now I know that God will do anything you ask."

Jesus told her, "Your brother will live again!"

Martha answered,
"I know that he will be raised to life on the last day,
when all the dead are raised."

Jesus then said,
"I am the one who raises the dead to life!
Everyone who has faith in me will live,
even if they die.
And everyone who lives because of faith in me
　　will never die.
Do you believe this?"

"Yes, Lord!" she replied.
"I believe that you are Christ, the Son of God.
You are the one we hoped would come into the world."

Many people had come to comfort Mary,
and when they saw her quickly leave the house,
they thought she was going out to the tomb to cry.
So they followed her.

Mary went to where Jesus was.
Then as soon as she saw him,
she kneeled at his feet and said,
"Lord, if you had been here,
my brother would not have died."

When Jesus saw that Mary and the people with her
　　were crying,
he was terribly upset and asked,
"Where have you put his body?"

continued

They replied, "Lord, come and you will see."

Jesus started crying, and the people said,
"See how much he loved Lazarus."

Some of them said, "He gives sight to the blind.
Why couldn't he have kept Lazarus from dying?"

Jesus was still terribly upset.
So he went to the tomb,
which was a cave with a stone rolled against the entrance.
Then he told the people to roll the stone away.
But Martha said, "Lord, you know that Lazarus
    has been dead four days,
and there will be a bad smell."

Jesus replied, "Didn't I tell you that if you had faith,
you would see the glory of God?"

After the stone had been rolled aside,
Jesus looked up toward heaven and prayed,
"Father, I thank you for answering my prayer.
I know that you always answer my prayers.
But I said this,
so that the people here would believe that you sent me."

When Jesus had finished praying, he shouted,
"Lazarus, come out!"
The man who had been dead came out.
His hands and feet were wrapped with strips of burial cloth,
and a cloth covered his face.

Jesus then told the people, "Untie him and let him go."

Many of the people who had come to visit Mary
    saw the things that Jesus did,
and they put their faith in him.

The gospel of the Lord.

PASSION SUNDAY
(Palm Sunday)
The Procession with Palms

GOSPEL | ✛ **A reading from the holy gospel according to Matthew**

Matthew 21:1-11

When Jesus and his disciples came near to Jerusalem,
he went to Bethphage on the Mount of Olives
   and sent two of his disciples on ahead.
He told them, "Go into the next village,
where you will at once find a donkey and her colt.
Untie the two donkeys and bring them to me.
If anyone asks why you are doing that, just say,
'The Lord needs them.'
Right away he will let you have the donkeys."

So God's promise came true,
just as the prophet had said,

> "Announce to the people of Jerusalem:
> 'Your king is coming to you!
> He is humble and rides on a donkey.
> He comes on the colt of a donkey.'"

The disciples left and did what Jesus had told them to do.
They brought the donkey and its colt
   and laid some clothes on their backs.
Then Jesus got on.

Blessed is the one who comes in the name of the Lord.

Many people spread clothes in the road,
while others put down branches
   which they had cut from trees.
Some people walked ahead of Jesus
   and others followed behind.
They were all shouting, "Hosanna for the Son of David!
God bless the one who comes in the name of the Lord.
Hooray for God in heaven above!"

When Jesus came to Jerusalem,
everyone in the city was excited and asked,
"Who can this be?"

The crowd answered,
"This is Jesus, the prophet from Nazareth in Galilee."

The gospel of the Lord.

Mass

The following readings may be used only when the celebration of the liturgy of the word for the children is held in a place apart from the main assembly.

FIRST READING | **A reading from the book of the prophet Isaiah**

Isaiah 50:6–7

I did not cover my face against insult and I know I will not be ashamed (third oracle of the Servant of the Lord).

I let them beat my back and pull out my beard.
I didn't turn aside when they made fun of me
 and spit in my face.

But the L<small>ORD</small> God keeps me from being embarrassed.
And I refuse to give up,
because I know I will never be ashamed.

The word of the Lord.

Responsorial Psalm

*R. My God, my God,
why have you abandoned me?*

*Everyone who sees me
makes fun and sneers.*

Psalm 22:7–8, 16c–17a and 18, 19 and 22 (2a)

*They shake their heads,
and say, "Trust the L<small>ORD</small>!
If you are his favorite,
let him protect you and keep you safe."*

*R. My God, my God,
why have you abandoned me?*

*My enemies have tied up
my hands and my feet.
I can count all my bones!
They took my clothes
and gambled for them.*

R. *My God, my God,
why have you abandoned me?*

*Don't stay far away, LORD!
My strength comes from you,
so hurry and help.
And when your people meet,
I will praise you, LORD.*

R. *My God, my God,
why have you abandoned me?*

Verse before the Gospel

Philippians 2:8–9

R. *Glory and praise to you,
Lord Jesus Christ.*

*Christ became obedient for us
even to death,
dying on the cross.
Therefore God raised him on high
and gave him a name
above all other names.*

R. *Glory and praise to you,
Lord Jesus Christ.*

| GOSPEL | **The passion of our Lord Jesus Christ according to Matthew** |

Matthew 27:11–54

Jesus was brought before Pilate the governor,
    who asked him,
"Are you the King of the Jews?"

"Those are your words!" Jesus answered.
And when the chief priests and leaders
    brought their charges against him,
he did not say a thing.

The passion of our Lord Jesus Christ.

Pilate asked him, "Don't you hear what crimes
    they say you have done?"
But Jesus did not say anything,
and the governor was greatly amazed.

During Passover the governor always freed
    a prisoner chosen by the people.
At that time a well-known terrorist named Jesus Barabbas
    was in jail.
So when the crowd came together, Pilate asked them,
"Which prisoner do you want me to set free?
Do you want Jesus Barabbas
    or Jesus who is called the Messiah?"
Pilate knew that the leaders had brought Jesus to him
because they were jealous.

While Pilate was judging the case,
his wife sent him a message.
It said, "Don't have anything to do with that innocent man.
I have had nightmares because of him."

But the chief priests and the leaders convinced the crowds
    to ask for Barabbas to be set free and for Jesus to be killed.
Pilate asked the crowd again,
"Which of these two men do you want me to set free?"

"Barabbas!" they replied.

Pilate asked them, "What am I to do with Jesus,
who is called the Messiah?"

They all yelled, "Nail him to a cross!"

Pilate answered, "But what crime has he done?"
"Nail him to a cross!" they yelled even louder.

Pilate saw that there was nothing he could do
   and that the people were starting to riot.
So he took some water
   and washed his hands in front of them and said,
"I won't have anything to do with killing this man.
You are the ones doing it!"

Everybody answered,
"We and our descendants will take the blame for his death!"

Pilate set Barabbas free.
Then he ordered his soldiers to beat Jesus with a whip
   and nail him to a cross.

The governor's soldiers led Jesus into the fortress
   and brought together the rest of the troops.
They stripped off Jesus' clothes
   and put a scarlet robe on him.
They made a crown out of thorn branches
   and placed it on his head,
and they put a stick in his right hand.
The soldiers kneeled down and pretended to worship him.
They made fun of him and shouted,
"Hey, you king of the Jews!"
Then they spit on him.
They took the stick from him
   and beat him on the head with it.

When the soldiers had finished making fun of Jesus,
they took off the robe.
They put his own clothes back on him
   and led him off to be nailed to a cross.
On the way they met a man from Cyrene named Simon,
and they forced him to carry Jesus' cross.

continued

They came to a place named Golgotha,
which means "Place of the Skull."
There they gave Jesus some wine
    mixed with a drug to ease the pain.
But when Jesus tasted what it was,
he refused to drink it.

The soldiers nailed Jesus to a cross
    and gambled to see who would get his clothes.
Then they sat down to guard him.
Above his head they put a sign
    that told why he was nailed there.
It said, "This is Jesus, the King of the Jews."
The soldiers also nailed two criminals on crosses,
    one to the right of Jesus and the other to his left.

People who passed by said terrible things about Jesus.
They shook their heads and shouted,
"So you're the one who claimed
    you could tear down the temple
    and build it again in three days!
If you are God's Son,
save yourself and come down from the cross!"

The chief priests, the leaders,
    and the teachers of the Law of Moses
    also made fun of Jesus.
They said, "He saved others, but he can't save himself.
If he is the king of Israel,
he should come down from the cross!
Then we will believe him.
He trusted God,
so let God save him, if he wants to.
He even said he was God's Son."

The two criminals also said cruel things to Jesus.

At noon the sky turned dark
   and stayed that way until three o'clock.
Then about that time Jesus shouted,

   "Eli, Eli, lema sabachthani?"
   which means, "My God, my God,
   why have you deserted me?"

Some of the people standing there heard Jesus and said,
"He's calling for Elijah."
One of them at once ran and grabbed a sponge.
He soaked it in wine,
then put it on a stick and held it up to Jesus.

Others said, "Wait!
Let's see if Elijah will come and save him."
Once again Jesus shouted,
and then he died.

At once the curtain in the temple was torn in two
   from top to bottom.
The earth shook, and rocks split apart.
Graves opened,
and many of God's people were raised to life.
Then after Jesus had risen to life,
they came out of their graves and went into the holy city,
where many people saw them.

The officer and the soldiers guarding Jesus
   felt the earthquake and saw everything else that happened.
They were frightened and said,
"This man really was God's Son!"

The gospel of the Lord.

SEASON OF EASTER

EASTER SUNDAY

The following readings may be used only when the celebration of the liturgy of the word for the children is held in a place apart from the main assembly.

FIRST READING

Acts 10:34a, 37–43

After Jesus was raised from the dead, we ate and drank with him.

A reading from the Acts of the Apostles

Peter said to Cornelius and his household:
"You surely know what happened everywhere in Judea.
It all began in Galilee after John had told everyone
 to be baptized.
God gave the Holy Spirit and power to Jesus from Nazareth.
He was with Jesus,
as he went around doing good
 and healing everyone
 who was under the power of the devil.
We all saw what Jesus did both in Israel
 and in the city of Jerusalem.

"Jesus was put to death on a cross.
But three days later,
God raised him to life and let him be seen.
Not everyone saw him.
He was seen only by us,
who ate and drank with him after he was raised from death.
We were the ones God chose to tell others about him.

"God told us to announce clearly to the people
that Jesus is the one he has chosen
 to judge the living and the dead.

"Every one of the prophets has said
that all who have faith in Jesus
 will have their sins forgiven in his name."

The word of the Lord.

Responsorial Psalm

R. *This is the day the Lord has made;*
let us rejoice and be glad.
or:
R. *Alleluia.*

Psalm 118:1–2, 15c–16ab and 17,
22–23 (24)

Tell the LORD
how thankful you are,
because he is kind
and always merciful.
Let Israel shout,
"God is always merciful!"

R. *This is the day the Lord has made;*
let us rejoice and be glad.
or:
R. *Alleluia.*

The LORD is powerful!
With his mighty arm
the LORD wins victories!
And so my life is safe,
and I will live to tell
what the LORD has done.

R. *This is the day the Lord has made;*
let us rejoice and be glad.
or:
R. *Alleluia.*

The stone that the builders
tossed aside
has now become
the most important stone.
The LORD has done this,
and it is amazing to us.

R. *This is the day the Lord has made;*
let us rejoice and be glad.
or:
R. *Alleluia.*

ONE

SECOND READING

Colossians 3:1–4

Look for the things that are in heaven, where Christ is.

A reading from the letter of Paul to the Colossians

Brothers and sisters:
You have been raised to life with Christ.
Now set your heart on what is in heaven,
where Christ rules at God's right side.
Think about what is up there,
not about what is here on earth.

You died, which means that your life is hidden with Christ,
who sits beside God.
Christ gives meaning to your life,
and when he appears,
you will also appear with him in glory.

The word of the Lord.

OR

TWO

SECOND READING

1 Corinthians 5:6b–8

Throw away the old yeast, that you may be new dough.

A reading from the first letter of Paul to the Corinthians

Brothers and sisters:
Don't you know how a little yeast can spread
   through the whole batch of dough?
Get rid of the old yeast!
Then you will be like fresh bread made without yeast,
and that is what you are.

Our Passover lamb is Christ,
who has already been sacrificed.
So don't celebrate the festival by being evil and sinful,
which is like serving bread made with yeast.
Be pure and truthful
   and celebrate by using bread made without yeast.

The word of the Lord.

Alleluia　　R. *Alleluia, alleluia.*

1 Corinthians 5:7b–8a　　*Christ has become*
our paschal sacrifice;
let us feast with joy in the Lord.

R. *Alleluia, alleluia.*

✛ **A reading from the holy gospel according to John**

On Sunday morning while it was still dark,
Mary Magdalene went to the tomb
　and saw that the stone had been rolled away
　from the entrance.
She ran to Simon Peter and to Jesus' favorite disciple
　and said,
"They have taken the Lord from the tomb!
We don't know where they have put him."

Peter and the other disciple started for the tomb.
They ran side by side,
until the other disciple ran faster than Peter
　and got there first.
He bent over and saw the strips of linen cloth
　lying inside the tomb,
but he did not go in.

When Simon Peter got there,
he went into the tomb and saw the strips of cloth.
He also saw the piece of cloth that had been used
　to cover Jesus' face.
It was rolled up and in a place by itself.
The disciple who got there first then went into the tomb,
and when he saw it, he believed.
At that time Peter and the other disciple did not know
　that the Scriptures said Jesus would rise to life.

The gospel of the Lord.

GOSPEL

John 20:1–9

The teaching of Scripture is that Jesus must rise from the dead.

SECOND SUNDAY OF EASTER

FIRST READING

Acts 2:42–47

All those who believed were equal and held everything in common.

A reading from the Acts of the Apostles

The followers of Jesus spent their time
   learning from the apostles,
and they were like family to each other.
They also broke bread and prayed together.

Everyone was amazed at the many miracles and wonders
   that the apostles worked.

All the Lord's followers often met together,
and they shared everything they had.
They would sell their property and possessions
   and give the money to whoever needed it.
Day after day they met together in the temple.
They broke bread together in different homes
   and shared their food happily and freely,
   while praising God.
Everyone liked them,
and each day the Lord added to their group
   others who were being saved.

The word of the Lord.

Responsorial Psalm   R. *Give thanks, for the Lord is good,*
God's love is everlasting.
or:
R. *Alleluia.*

Psalm 118:2–4, 22–24
(1)

Let Israel shout,
"God is always merciful!"
Let the family of Aaron
the priest shout,
"God is always merciful!"
Let every true worshiper
of the LORD *shout,*
"God is always merciful!"

R. *Give thanks, for the Lord is good,*
God's love is everlasting.
or:
R. *Alleluia.*

The stone that the builders
tossed aside
has now become
the most important stone.
The LORD *has done this,*
and it is amazing to us.
This day belongs to the LORD!
Let's celebrate and be glad today.

R. *Give thanks, for the Lord is good,*
God's love is everlasting.
or:
R. *Alleluia.*

Second Reading

1 Peter 1:3–4

God has given us a new birth as his children, by raising Jesus Christ from the dead.

A reading from the first letter of Peter

Brothers and sisters:
Praise God, the Father of our Lord Jesus Christ.
God is so good,
and by raising Jesus from death,
he has given us new life and a hope that lives on.

God has something stored up for you in heaven,
where it will never decay or be ruined or disappear.

The word of the Lord.

Alleluia

John 20:29

R. Alleluia, alleluia.

*You believe in me, Thomas,
because you have seen me;
happy those who have not seen me,
but still believe!*

R. Alleluia, alleluia.

Gospel

John 20:19–29

After eight days Jesus came in and stood among them.

✛ A reading from the holy gospel according to John

The disciples were afraid of the Jewish leaders,
and on the evening of that same Sunday
   they locked themselves in a room.
Suddenly, Jesus appeared in the middle of the group.
He greeted them and showed them his hands and his side.
When the disciples saw the Lord,
they became very happy.

After Jesus had greeted them again, he said,
"I am sending you, just as the Father has sent me."
Then he breathed on them and said,
"Receive the Holy Spirit.
If you forgive anyone's sins,
they will be forgiven.
But if you don't forgive their sins,
they will not be forgiven."

Although Thomas the Twin was one of the twelve disciples,
he was not with the others when Jesus appeared to them.
So they told him, "We have seen the Lord!"

But Thomas said,
   "First, I must see the nail scars in his hands
   and touch them with my finger.
I must put my hand where the spear went into his side.
I won't believe unless I do this!"

A week later the disciples were together again.
This time Thomas was with them.
Jesus came in while the doors were still locked
   and stood in the middle of the group.
He greeted his disciples and said to Thomas,
"Put your finger here and look at my hands!
Put your hand into my side.
Stop doubting and have faith!"

Thomas replied, "You are my Lord and my God!"

Jesus said, "Thomas, do you have faith
   because you have seen me?
The people who have faith in me without seeing me
   are the ones who are really blessed!"

The gospel of the Lord.

THIRD SUNDAY OF EASTER

FIRST READING

Acts 2:14, 22–24

It was impossible for Jesus to be held by the power of Hades.

A reading from the Acts of the Apostles

On the day of Pentecost,
Peter stood with the eleven apostles
 and spoke in a loud and clear voice to the crowd:

"Friends and everyone else living in Jerusalem,
listen carefully to what I have to say!

"Now, listen to what I have to say
 about Jesus from Nazareth.
God proved that he sent Jesus to you
 by having him work miracles, wonders, and signs.
All of you know this.

"God had already planned and decided
 that Jesus would be handed over to you.
So you took him and had evil men
 put him to death on a cross.

"But God set him free from death and raised him to life.
Death could not hold him in its power."

The word of the Lord.

Responsorial Psalm   R. *I love you, Lord, my strength.*
or:
R. *Alleluia.*

Psalm 18:1–2, 46 and 50ab
(2)

*I love you, L*ORD *God,*
and you make me strong.
You are my mighty rock,
my fortress, my protector,
the rock where I am safe,
my shield, my powerful weapon,
and my place of shelter.

R. *I love you, Lord, my strength.*
or:
R. *Alleluia.*

*You are the living L*ORD*!*
I will praise you.
You are a mighty rock.
I will honor you
for keeping me safe.
You give glorious victories
to your chosen king.

R. *I love you, Lord, my strength.*
or:
R. *Alleluia.*

Alleluia   R. *Alleluia, alleluia.*

See Luke 24:32   *Lord Jesus,*
make your word plain to us;
make our hearts burn with love
when you speak.

R. *Alleluia, alleluia.*

GOSPEL

Luke 24:13–35

They recognized Jesus in the breaking of the bread.

✚ **A reading from the holy gospel according to Luke**

Two of Jesus' disciples were going to the village of Emmaus,
which was about seven miles from Jerusalem.
As they were talking and thinking
    about what had happened,
Jesus came near and started walking along beside them.
But they did not know who he was.

Jesus asked them,
    "What were you talking about as you walked along?"

The two of them stood there looking sad and gloomy.
Then the one named Cleopas asked Jesus,
"Are you the only person from Jerusalem
who didn't know what was happening there
    these last few days?"

"What do you mean?" Jesus asked.

They answered:
"Those things that happened to Jesus from Nazareth.
By what he did and said
he showed that he was a powerful prophet,
who pleased God and all the people.
Then the chief priests and our leaders
    had him arrested and sentenced to die on a cross.
We had hoped that he would be the one to set Israel free!

"But it has already been three days since all this happened.
Some women in our group surprised us.
They had gone to the tomb early in the morning,
but did not find the body of Jesus.
They came back,
saying that they had seen a vision of angels
who told them that he is alive.
Some men from our group went to the tomb
    and found it just as the women had said.
But they didn't see Jesus either."

Then Jesus asked the two disciples,
"Why can't you understand?
How can you be so slow to believe all that the prophets said?
Didn't you know that the Messiah would have to suffer
   before he was given his glory?"

Jesus then explained everything written about himself
   in the Scriptures,
beginning with the Law of Moses and the Books of the Prophets.

When the two of them came near the village
   where they were going,
Jesus seemed to be going farther.
They begged him, "Stay with us!
It's already late, and the sun is going down."
So Jesus went into the house to stay with them.

After Jesus sat down to eat,
he took some bread.
He blessed it and broke it.
Then he gave it to them.
At once they knew who he was,
but he disappeared.

They said to each other,
"When he talked with us along the road
   and explained the Scriptures to us,
didn't it warm our hearts?"
So they got right up and returned to Jerusalem.

The two disciples
   found the eleven apostles and the others gathered together.
And they learned from the group
   that the Lord was really alive and had appeared to Peter.

Then the disciples from Emmaus
   told what happened on the road
and how they knew he was the Lord
when he broke the bread.

The gospel of the Lord.

FOURTH SUNDAY OF EASTER

FIRST READING | A reading from the Acts of the Apostles

Acts 2:14a, 36–41

On the day of Pentecost,
Peter stood with the eleven apostles
   and spoke in a loud and clear voice to the crowd:

"Everyone in Israel should know for certain
   that God has made Jesus both Lord and Christ,
even though you put him to death on a cross."

God has made Jesus both Lord and Christ.

When the people heard this, they were very upset.
They asked Peter and the other apostles,
"Friends, what shall we do?"

Peter said, "Turn back to God!
Be baptized in the name of Jesus Christ,
so that your sins will be forgiven.
Then you will be given the Holy Spirit.
This promise is for you and your children.
It is for everyone our Lord God will choose,
no matter where they live."

Peter told the people many other things as well.
Then he said, "I beg you to save yourselves
   from what will happen to all these evil people."

On that day about three thousand believed his message
   and were baptized.

The word of the Lord.

FOURTH SUNDAY OF EASTER

Responsorial Psalm   R. *The Lord is my shepherd;*
there is nothing I shall want.
or:
R. Alleluia.

Psalm 23:1–3a, 3b–4, 6
(1)

You, LORD, are my shepherd.
I will never be in need.
You let me rest in fields of green grass.
You lead me to streams of peaceful water,
and you refresh my life.

R. *The Lord is my shepherd;*
there is nothing I shall want.
or:
R. Alleluia.

You are true to your name,
and you lead me
along the right paths.
I may walk through valleys
as dark as death,
but I won't be afraid.
You are with me,
and your shepherd's rod
makes me feel safe.

R. *The Lord is my shepherd;*
there is nothing I shall want.
or:
R. Alleluia.

Your kindness and love
will always be with me
each day of my life,
and I will live forever
in your house, LORD.

R. *The Lord is my shepherd;*
there is nothing I shall want.
or:
R. Alleluia.

Alleluia R. *Alleluia, alleluia.*

John 10:14 *I am the good shepherd, says the Lord;*
I know my sheep, and mine know me.

R. *Alleluia, alleluia.*

GOSPEL ✠ **A reading from the holy gospel according to John**

John 10:1–10

Jesus said to his disciples:
"I tell you for certain
   that only thieves and robbers climb over the fence
   instead of going in through the gate to the sheep pen.
But the gatekeeper opens the gate for the shepherd,
and he goes in through it.

I am the gate of the sheepfold.

The sheep know their shepherd's voice.
He calls each of them by name and leads them out.

"When he has led out all of his sheep,
he walks in front of them,
and they follow, because they know his voice.
The sheep will not follow strangers.
They don't recognize a stranger's voice,
and they run away."

Jesus told the people this story.
But they did not understand what he was talking about.

Then Jesus said:
"I tell you for certain that I am the gate for the sheep.
Everyone who came before me was a thief or a robber,
and the sheep did not listen to any of them.
I am the gate.
All who come in through me will be saved.
Through me they will come and go and find pasture.

"A thief comes only to rob, kill, and destroy.
I came so that everyone would have life,
   and have it in its fullest."

The gospel of the Lord.

FIFTH SUNDAY OF EASTER

FIRST READING

A reading from the Acts of the Apostles

Acts 6:1–7a

A lot of people were becoming followers of the Lord.
But some of the ones who spoke Greek started complaining
 about the ones who spoke Aramaic.
They complained that the Greek-speaking widows
 were not given their share
 when the food supplies were handed out each day.

They chose seven men filled with the Spirit.

The twelve apostles
 called the whole group of followers together and said,
"We should not give up preaching God's message
 in order to serve at tables.
My friends, choose seven men who are respected and wise
 and filled with God's Spirit.
We will put them in charge of these things.
We can spend our time praying and serving God
 by preaching."

This suggestion pleased everyone,
and they began by choosing Stephen.
He had great faith and was filled with the Holy Spirit.

Then they chose Philip, Prochorus, Nicanor, Timon,
 Parmenas, and also Nicolaus,
 who worshiped with the Jewish people in Antioch.
These men were brought to the apostles.
Then the apostles prayed and placed their hands on the men
 to show that they had been chosen to do this work.

God's message spread,
and many more people in Jerusalem became followers.

The word of the Lord.

Responsorial Psalm

R. *You open your hand to feed us, Lord;*
you answer all our needs.
or:
R. *Alleluia.*

Psalm 145:10–11, 15–16, 17–18
(16)

All creation will thank you,
and your loyal people will praise you.
They will tell about
your marvelous kingdom and your power.

R. *You open your hand to feed us, Lord;*
you answer all our needs.
or:
R. *Alleluia.*

Everyone depends on you,
and when the time is right,
you provide them with food.
By your own hand you satisfy
the desires of all who live.

R. *You open your hand to feed us, Lord;*
you answer all our needs.
or:
R. *Alleluia.*

Our LORD, *everything you do*
is kind and thoughtful,
and you are near to everyone
whose prayers are sincere.

R. *You open your hand to feed us, Lord;*
you answer all our needs.
or:
R. *Alleluia.*

Alleluia

R. Alleluia, alleluia.

John 14:6

I am the way, the truth, and the life,
says the Lord;
no one comes to the Father,
except through me.

R. Alleluia, alleluia.

GOSPEL

✠ **A reading from the holy gospel according to John**

John 14:1–12

Jesus said to his disciples,
"Don't be worried!
Have faith in God and have faith in me.
There are many rooms in my Father's house.
I wouldn't tell you this, unless it was true.
I am going there to prepare a place for each of you.

I am the way, the truth, and the life.

After I have done this,
I will come back and take you with me.
Then we will be together.
You know the way to where I am going."

Thomas said, "Lord, we don't even know
    where you are going!
How can we know the way?"

"I am the way, the truth, and the life!" Jesus answered.
"Without me, no one can go to the Father.
If you had known me,
you would have known the Father.
But from now on, you do know him,
and you have seen him."

Philip said, "Lord, show us the Father.
That is all we need."

Jesus replied:
"Philip, I have been with you for a long time.
Don't you know who I am?
If you have seen me, you have seen the Father.
How can you ask me to show you the Father?
Don't you believe that I am one with the Father
    and that the Father is one with me?
What I say is not said on my own.
The Father who lives in me does these things.

"Have faith in me when I say that the Father is one with me
    and that I am one with the Father.
Or else have faith in me simply because of the things I do.

"I tell you for certain that if you have faith in me,
you will do the same things that I am doing.
You will do even greater things,
now that I am going back to the Father."

The gospel of the Lord.

SIXTH SUNDAY OF EASTER

FIRST READING

Acts 8:5–8, 14–17

Peter and John laid hands on them, and they received the Holy Spirit.

A reading from the Acts of the Apostles

Philip went to the town of Samaria
  and told the people about Christ.
They crowded around Philip
because they were eager to hear what he was saying
  and to see him work miracles.
Many people with evil spirits were healed,
and the spirits went out of them with a shout.
A lot of crippled and lame people were also healed.
Everyone in that city was very glad
  because of what was happening.

When the apostles in Jerusalem
  heard that some people in Samaria
  had accepted God's message,
they sent Peter and John.
When the two apostles arrived,
they prayed that the people would be given the Holy Spirit.

Before this, the Holy Spirit had not been given
  to anyone in Samaria
  though some of them had been baptized
  in the name of the Lord Jesus.

Peter and John then placed their hands
  on everyone who had faith in the Lord,
and they were given the Holy Spirit.

The word of the Lord.

Responsorial Psalm

R. Let all the earth
cry out to God with joy.
or:
R. Alleluia.

Psalm 66:1–3ab, 4–5, 16 and 20
(1)

Tell everyone on this earth
to shout praises to God!
Sing about his glorious name.
Honor him with praises.
Say to God, "Everything you do
is fearsome!"

R. Let all the earth
cry out to God with joy.
or:
R. Alleluia.

"You are worshiped by everyone!
We all sing praises to you."
Come and see the fearsome things
our God has done!

R. Let all the earth
cry out to God with joy.
or:
R. Alleluia.

All who worship God,
come here and listen;
I will tell you everything
God has done for me.
Let's praise God!
He listened when I prayed,
and he is always kind.

R. Let all the earth
cry out to God with joy.
or:
R. Alleluia.

Alleluia   R. Alleluia, alleluia.

John 14:23

All who love me will keep my words,
and my Father will love them,
and we will come to them.

R. Alleluia, alleluia.

GOSPEL

John 14:15–21

I shall ask the Father and he will give you another Advocate.

✠ **A reading from the holy gospel according to John**

Jesus said to his disciples:
"If you love me, you will do as I command.
Then I will ask the Father to send you the Holy Spirit
 who will help you and always be with you.
The Spirit will show you what is true.

"The people of this world cannot accept the Spirit,
because they don't see or know him.
But you know the Spirit, who is with you
 and will keep on living in you.

"I won't leave you like orphans.
I will come back to you.
In a little while the people of this world
 won't be able to see me,
but you will see me.
And because I live, you will live.
Then you will know that I am one with the Father.
You will know that you are one with me,
and I am one with you.

"If you love me, you will do what I have said,
and my Father will love you.
I will also love you and show you what I am like."

The gospel of the Lord.

SIXTH SUNDAY OF EASTER

THE ASCENSION OF THE LORD

The following readings may be used only when the celebration of the liturgy of the word for the children is held in a place apart from the main assembly.

FIRST READING

Acts 1:8–11

Why are you standing here looking at the sky? Jesus has been taken into heaven.

A reading from the Acts of the Apostles

Jesus told his disciples:
"The Holy Spirit will come upon you and give you power.
Then you will tell everyone about me in Jerusalem,
 in all Judea, in Samaria, and everywhere in the world."

After Jesus had said this and while they were watching,
he was taken up into a cloud.
They could not see him, but as he went up,
they kept looking up into the sky.

Suddenly two men dressed in white clothes
 were standing there beside them.
They said, "Why are you men from Galilee
 standing here and looking up into the sky?
Jesus has been taken to heaven.
But he will come back in the same way
 that you have seen him go."

The word of the Lord.

Responsorial Psalm R. *God mounts the throne*
to shouts of joy.
or:
R. Alleluia.

Psalm 47:1–2, 5–6, 7–8
(6a)

All of you nations,
clap your hands and shout
joyful praises to God.
The LORD Most High is fearsome,
the ruler of all the earth.

R. God mounts the throne
to shouts of joy.
or:
R. Alleluia.

God goes up to his throne,
as people shout
and trumpets blast.
Sing praises to God our King.

R. God mounts the throne
to shouts of joy.
or:
R. Alleluia.

God is ruler of all the earth!
Praise God with songs.
God rules the nations
from his sacred throne.

R. God mounts the throne
to shouts of joy.
or:
R. Alleluia.

SECOND READING

Ephesians 1:17–21

God seated Jesus at his right hand in heaven.

A reading from the letter of Paul to the Ephesians

Brothers and sisters:
I ask the glorious Father and God of our Lord Jesus Christ
   to give you his Spirit.
The Spirit will make you wise and let you understand
   what it means to know God.

My prayer is that light will flood your hearts
   and that you will understand the hope
   that was given to you when God chose you.
Then you will discover the glorious blessings
   that will be yours together with all of God's people.

I want you to know about the great and mighty power
   that God has for us followers.
It is the same wonderful power he used
   when he raised Christ from death
   and let him sit at his right side in heaven.
There Christ rules over all forces, authorities,
   powers, and rulers.
He rules over all beings in this world
   and will rule in the future world as well.

The word of the Lord.

THE ASCENSION OF THE LORD

Alleluia *R. Alleluia, alleluia.*

Matthew 28:19a, 20b *Go and teach all people my gospel;*
I am with you always,
until the end of the world.

R. Alleluia, alleluia.

✠ **A reading from the holy gospel according to Matthew**

Jesus' eleven disciples went to a mountain in Galilee,
where Jesus had told them to meet him.
They saw him and worshiped him,
but some of them doubted.

Jesus came to them and said:
"I have been given all authority in heaven and on earth!
Go to the people of all nations and make them my disciples.
Baptize them in the name of the Father,
    the Son, and the Holy Spirit,
and teach them to do everything I have told you.

"I will be with you always,
even until the end of the world."

The gospel of the Lord.

GOSPEL

Matthew 28:16–20

All authority
in heaven and on earth
has been given to me.

SEVENTH SUNDAY OF EASTER

FIRST READING

Acts 1:12–14

They all joined together in continuous prayer in the upper room.

A reading from the Acts of the Apostles

The Mount of Olives
   was about half a mile from Jerusalem.
The apostles who had gone there were Peter,
   John, James, Andrew,
   Philip, Thomas, Bartholomew, Matthew,
   James the son of Alphaeus,
   Simon, known as the Eager One,
   and Judas the son of James.

After the apostles returned to the city,
   they went upstairs to the room where they had been staying.

The apostles often met together
   and prayed with a single purpose in mind.
The women and Mary the mother of Jesus
   would meet with them,
and so would his brothers.

The word of the Lord.

Responsorial Psalm

R. *I believe that I shall see the good things of the Lord.*
or:
R. *Alleluia.*

Psalm 27:1, 4abc, 7–8 (13a)

You, LORD, are the light that keeps me safe.
I am not afraid of anyone.
You protect me,
and I have no fears.

R. *I believe that I shall see the good things of the Lord.*
or:
R. *Alleluia.*

I ask only one thing, LORD:
Let me live in your house every day of my life.

R. *I believe that I shall see the good things of the Lord.*
or:
R. *Alleluia.*

Please listen when I pray!
Have pity. Answer my prayer.
My heart tells me to pray.
I am eager to see your face.

R. *I believe that I shall see the good things of the Lord.*
or:
R. *Alleluia.*

SECOND READING

1 Peter 4:13–16

It is a blessing for you when they insult you for bearing the name of Christ.

A reading from the first letter of Peter

Brothers and sisters:
Be glad for the chance to suffer as Christ suffered.
It will prepare you for even greater happiness
    when he makes his glorious return.

Count it a blessing when you suffer for being a Christian.
This shows that God's glorious Spirit is with you.
But you deserve to suffer if you are a murderer, a thief,
    a crook, or a busybody.
Don't be ashamed to suffer for being a Christian.
Praise God that you belong to him.

The word of the Lord.

Alleluia

See John 14:18

R. *Alleluia, alleluia.*

The Lord says:
I will not leave you orphans.
I will come back to you,
and your hearts will rejoice.

R. *Alleluia, alleluia.*

✚ A reading from the holy gospel according to John

Jesus prayed to God:
"You have given me some followers from this world,
and I have shown them what you are like.

"They were yours,
but you gave them to me,
and they have obeyed you.
They know that you gave me everything I have.

"I told my followers what you told me,
and they accepted it.
They know that I came from you,
and they believe that you are the one who sent me.

"I am praying for them,
but not for those who belong to this world.
My followers belong to you,
and I am praying for them."

The gospel of the Lord.

GOSPEL

John 17:6–9

*My followers belong to you,
and I am praying for them.*

PENTECOST SUNDAY

The following readings may be used only when the celebration of the liturgy of the word for the children is held in a place apart from the main assembly.

FIRST READING

Acts 2:1–11

They were all filled with the Holy Spirit, and began to speak different languages.

A reading from the Acts of the Apostles

On the day of Pentecost
   all the Lord's followers were together in one place.
Suddenly there was a noise from heaven
   like the sound of a mighty wind!
It filled the house where they were meeting.
Then they saw what looked like fiery tongues
   moving in all directions,
and a tongue came and settled on each person there.
The Holy Spirit took control of everyone,
and they began speaking
   whatever languages the Spirit let them speak.

Many religious Jews from every country in the world
   were living in Jerusalem.
And when they heard this noise, a crowd gathered.
But they were surprised,
because they were hearing everything
   in their own languages.

They were excited and amazed, and said:
"Don't all these who are speaking come from Galilee?
Then why do we each hear them speaking
   our very own languages?
Some of us are from Parthia, Media, and Elam.
Others are from Mesopotamia, Judea,
   Cappadocia, Pontus, Asia,
   Phrygia, Pamphylia, Egypt,
   parts of Libya near Cyrene,
   Rome, Crete, and Arabia.
Some of us were born Jews,
and others of us have chosen to be Jews.
Yet we all hear them using our own languages
   to tell the wonderful things God has done."

The word of the Lord.

Responsorial Psalm R. Lord, send out your Spirit,
and renew the face of the earth.
or:
R. Alleluia.

Psalm 104:1abc and 24, 30–31
(see 30)

I praise you, LORD God,
with all my heart.
You are glorious and majestic.
Our LORD, by your wisdom
you made so many things;
the whole earth is covered
with your living creatures.

R. Lord, send out your Spirit,
and renew the face of the earth.
or:
R. Alleluia.

You created all of them
by your Spirit,
and you give new life
to the earth.
Our LORD, we pray
that your glory will last for ever
and that you will be pleased
with what you have done.

R. Lord, send out your Spirit,
and renew the face of the earth.
or:
R. Alleluia.

SECOND READING

1 Corinthians 12:4–7, 12–13

In the one Spirit we were all baptized into one body.

A reading from the first letter of Paul to the Corinthians

Brothers and sisters:
There are different kinds of spiritual gifts,
but they all come from the same Spirit.
There are different ways to serve the same Lord,
and we can each do different things.
Yet the same God works in all of us
   and helps us in everything we do.

The Spirit has given each of us a special way
   of serving others.

The body of Christ has many different parts,
   just as any other body does.
Some of us are Jews,
and others are Gentiles.
Some of us are slaves,
and others are free.
But God's Spirit baptized each of us
   and made us part of the body of Christ.
Now we each drink from that same Spirit.

The word of the Lord.

Alleluia

R. *Alleluia, alleluia.*

Come, Holy Spirit,
fill the hearts of your faithful
and kindle in them
the fire of your love.

R. *Alleluia, alleluia.*

GOSPEL

John 20:19–23

✛ A reading from the holy gospel according to John

The disciples were afraid of the Jewish leaders,
and on the evening of that same Sunday
  they locked themselves in a room.
Suddenly, Jesus appeared in the middle of the group.
He greeted them and showed them his hands and his side.
When the disciples saw the Lord,
they became very happy.

After Jesus had greeted them again, he said,
"I am sending you, just as the Father has sent me."
Then he breathed on them and said,
"Receive the Holy Spirit.
If you forgive anyone's sins,
they will be forgiven.
But if you don't forgive their sins,
they will not be forgiven."

The gospel of the Lord.

As the Father sent me, so I send you. Receive the Holy Spirit.

ORDINARY TIME

SECOND SUNDAY IN ORDINARY TIME

FIRST READING

Isaiah 49:3, 5–6

I will make you the light of the nations, so that my salvation may reach to the ends of the earth.

A reading from the book of the prophet Isaiah

The LORD said to me,
"Israel, you are my servant,
and because of you I will be highly honored."

Even before I was born,
the LORD chose me to serve him
    and to bring back the people of Israel.
The LORD God has honored me and made me strong.

Now the LORD says to me,
"It isn't enough for you to be merely my servant.
You must do more than lead back
    those from the tribes of Israel who have survived.
I have placed you here as a light for the Gentiles.
You are to take my saving power everywhere on earth."

The word of the Lord.

Responsorial Psalm

Psalm 40:1 and 3ab, 8 and 11
(8a and 9a)

R. Here am I, Lord;
I come to do your will.

I patiently waited, LORD,
for you to hear my prayer.
You listened
and you gave me a new song,
a song of praise to you.

R. Here am I, Lord;
I come to do your will.

"I enjoy pleasing you.
Your Law is in my heart."
You, LORD, never fail
to have pity on me;
your love and faithfulness
always keep me secure.

R. Here am I, Lord;
I come to do your will.

Alleluia

R. Alleluia, alleluia.

John 1:14a, 12a

*The Word of God became flesh
and dwelt among us.
He enabled those who accepted him
to become the children of God.*

R. Alleluia, alleluia.

GOSPEL

✠ **A reading from the holy gospel according to John**

John 1:29–34

John saw Jesus coming toward him and said:
"Here is the Lamb of God
   who takes away the sin of the world!
He is the one I told you about when I said,

This is the Lamb of God who takes away the sins of the world.

   'Someone else will come.
   He is greater than I am,
   because he was alive before I was born.'

"I didn't know who he was.
But I came to baptize you with water,
so that everyone in Israel would see him.

"I was there and saw the Spirit come down on him
    like a dove from heaven.
And the Spirit stayed on him.
Before this I didn't know who he was.
But the one who sent me to baptize with water had told me,
'You will see the Spirit come down and stay on someone.
Then you will know that he is the one
    who will baptize with the Holy Spirit.'

"I saw this happen,
and I tell you that he is the Son of God."

The gospel of the Lord.

THIRD SUNDAY IN ORDINARY TIME

FIRST READING

A reading from the book of the prophet Isaiah

Isaiah 9:2–4

The people have seen a great light.

Those who walked in the dark have seen a bright light.
And it shines upon everyone
   who lives in the land of darkest shadows.

Our LORD, you have made your nation stronger.
Because of you, its people are glad and celebrate
   like workers at harvest time
   or soldiers dividing what they have taken.

You have broken the power
   of those who oppressed and enslaved your people.
You have rescued them as you did from Midian.

The word of the Lord.

Responsorial Psalm R. *The Lord is my light and my salvation.*

*You, LORD, are the light
that keeps me safe.
I am not afraid of anyone.*

*Psalm 27:1, 4abc
(1a)*

*You protect me,
and I have no fears.*

R. *The Lord is my light and my salvation.*

*I ask only one thing, LORD:
Let me live in your house
every day of my life.*

R. *The Lord is my light and my salvation.*

Second Reading

1 Corinthians 1:10–13, 17

I appeal to you, my brothers and sisters, there should not be serious differences between you.

A reading from the first letter of Paul to the Corinthians

My dear friends,
as a follower of our Lord Jesus Christ,
I beg you to get along with each other.
Don't take sides.
Always try to agree in what you think.

Several people from Chloe's family
   have already reported to me
that you keep arguing with each other.

They have said that some of you claim to follow me,
while others claim to follow Apollos or Peter or Christ.

Has Christ been divided up?
Was I nailed to a cross for you?
Were you baptized in my name?

Christ did not send me to baptize.
He sent me to tell the good news without using big words
   that would make the cross of Christ lose its power.

The word of the Lord.

Alleluia

See Matthew 4:23

R. *Alleluia, alleluia.*

*Jesus preached the good news
of the kingdom
and healed all who were sick.*

R. *Alleluia, alleluia.*

GOSPEL

Matthew 4:17–23

✚ **A reading from the holy gospel according to Matthew**

Jesus started preaching, "Turn back to God!
The kingdom of heaven will soon be here."

While Jesus was walking along the shore of Lake Galilee,
he saw two brothers.
One was Simon, also known as Peter,
and the other was Andrew.
They were fishermen,
   and they were casting their net into the lake.

Come with me.

Jesus said to them, "Come with me!
I will teach you how to bring in people instead of fish."
Right then the two brothers dropped their nets
   and went with him.

Jesus walked on until he saw James and John,
   the sons of Zebedee.
They were in a boat with their father, mending their nets.
Jesus asked them to come with him too.
Right away they left the boat and their father
   and went with Jesus.

Jesus went all over Galilee,
   teaching in the Jewish meeting places
   and preaching the good news about God's kingdom.

He also healed every kind of disease and sickness.

The gospel of the Lord.

FOURTH SUNDAY IN ORDINARY TIME

FIRST READING

Zephaniah 2:3; 3:12–13

In your midst I will leave a humble and a lowly people.

A reading from the book of the prophet Zephaniah

If you humbly obey the LORD,
then come and worship him.
If you do right and are humble,
you might be safe on that day
   when the LORD shows his anger.
I won't destroy any of you that are truly humble
   and come to me for safety.
The people of Israel who survive will live right
   and refuse to tell lies.
They will eat in peace,
and no one will bother them.

The word of the Lord.

Responsorial Psalm

R. *Blessed are the poor in spirit;*
the kingdom of heaven is theirs!

God always keeps his word.
He gives justice to the poor
and food to the hungry.

Psalm 146:6d–7ab, 7c–9a
(Matthew 5:3)

R. *Blessed are the poor in spirit;*
the kingdom of heaven is theirs!

The LORD sets prisoners free
and heals blind eyes.
He gives a helping hand
to everyone who falls.
The LORD loves good people
and looks after strangers.

R. *Blessed are the poor in spirit;*
the kingdom of heaven is theirs!

Second Reading

1 Corinthians 1:26–31

God has chosen what is weak by human reckoning.

A reading from the first letter of Paul to the Corinthians

My dear friends,
remember what you were when God chose you.
The people of this world
   didn't think that many of you were wise.
Only a few of you were in places of power,
and not many of you came from important families.

But God chose the foolish things of this world
   to put the wise to shame.
He chose the weak things of this world
   to put the powerful to shame.

What the world thinks is worthless, useless,
   and nothing at all is what God has used
   to destroy what the world considers important.
God did all this to keep anyone from bragging to him.
You are God's children.
He sent Christ Jesus to save us
   and to make us wise, acceptable, and holy.
So if you want to brag,
do what the Scriptures say and brag about the Lord.

The word of the Lord.

Alleluia

Matthew 5:12a

R. Alleluia, alleluia.

*Rejoice and be glad;
your reward will be great in heaven.*

R. Alleluia, alleluia.

Gospel

Matthew 5:1–12ab

✠ A reading from the holy gospel according to Matthew

When Jesus saw the crowds,
he went up on the side of a mountain and sat down.

Jesus' disciples gathered around him, and he taught them:

"God blesses those people who depend only on him.
They belong to the kingdom of heaven!

"God blesses those people who grieve.
They will find comfort!

"God blesses those people who are humble.
The earth will belong to them!

"God blesses those people who want to obey him
    more than to eat or drink.
They will be given what they want!

"God blesses those people who are merciful.
They will be treated with mercy!

"God blesses those people whose hearts are pure.
They will see him!

"God blesses those people who make peace.
They will be called his children!

"God blesses those people who are treated badly
    for doing right.
They belong to the kingdom of heaven.

"God will bless you when people insult you, mistreat you,
    and tell all kinds of evil lies about you because of me.
Be happy and excited!
You will have a great reward in heaven."

The gospel of the Lord.

Blessed are the poor in spirit.

FIFTH SUNDAY IN ORDINARY TIME

First Reading

Isaiah 58:7–10

Your light will shine like the dawn.

A reading from the book of the prophet Isaiah

The LORD says this:
Share your food with everyone who is hungry,
and share your home with the poor and homeless.
Give clothes to all in need
and don't turn away your own relatives.

Then your light will shine like the dawning sun,
and you will quickly heal.
Your honesty will protect you as you advance,
and the glory of the LORD will defend you from behind.
Then you will call for help,
and the LORD will answer, "Here I am!"

Don't oppress others or falsely accuse them
   or say cruel things.
Give your food to the hungry,
and care for the helpless.
Then your light will shine in the darkness,
and your darkest hour will be like the noonday sun.

The word of the Lord.

Responsorial Psalm R. *A light rises in the darkness*
for the upright.
or:
R. Alleluia.

Psalm 112:4–5, 8ab and 9
(4a)

Those who worship the LORD
will be so kind and merciful and good,
that they will be a light
in the dark for others
who do the right thing.
Life will go well for those
who freely lend
and are honest in business.

R. *A light rises in the darkness*
for the upright.
or:
R. Alleluia.

They are dependable
and not afraid.
They will always be remembered
and greatly praised,
because they were kind
and freely gave to the poor.

R. *A light rises in the darkness*
for the upright.
or:
R. Alleluia.

Second Reading

1 Corinthians 2:1–5

I have announced to you knowledge of Christ crucified.

A reading from the first letter of Paul to the Corinthians

Brothers and sisters:
When I came and told you
   the mystery that God had shared with us,
I didn't use big words or try to sound wise.
In fact, while I was with you,
I made up my mind to speak only about Jesus Christ,
who had been nailed to a cross.

At first, I was weak and trembling with fear.
When I talked with you or preached,
I didn't try to prove anything by sounding wise.
I simply let God's Spirit show his power.
That way you would have faith because of God's power
   and not because of human wisdom.

The word of the Lord.

Alleluia

John 8:12

R. *Alleluia, alleluia.*

*I am the light of the world,
says the Lord;
whoever follows me
will have the light of life.*

R. *Alleluia, alleluia.*

FIFTH SUNDAY IN ORDINARY TIME

✚ A reading from the holy gospel according to Matthew

Jesus said to his disciples:
"You are like salt for everyone on earth.
But if salt no longer tastes like salt,
how can it make food salty?
All it is good for is to be thrown out and walked on.

"You are like light for the whole world.
A city built on top of a hill cannot be hidden,
and no one would light a lamp and put it under a clay pot.
A lamp is placed on a lamp stand,
where it can give light to everyone in the house.
Make your light shine,
so that others will see the good that you do
 and will praise your Father in heaven."

The gospel of the Lord.

GOSPEL

Matthew 5:13–16

*You are
the light of the world.*

SIXTH SUNDAY IN ORDINARY TIME

FIRST READING

Sirach 15:15–20

The Lord never commanded anyone to be godless.

A reading from the book of Sirach

If you really want to,
you can faithfully obey the Lord's commands.
The Lord gives you the choice between fire and water.
Take the one you want.
You can also choose between life and death.
The one you want is yours.
The Lord is very wise.
He can do anything,
and he sees everything.
The Lord watches over everyone who respects him,
and he knows everything that anyone does.
The Lord did not command us to sin and do wrong.

The word of the Lord.

Responsorial Psalm

*R. Happy are they
who follow the law of the Lord!*

Psalm 119:1–2, 4–5, 33–34
(1b)

*Our LORD, you bless everyone
who lives right and obeys your Law.
You bless all of those
who follow your commands
from deep in their hearts.*

*R. Happy are they
who follow the law of the Lord!*

*You have ordered us always
to obey your teachings;
I don't ever want to stray
from your laws.*

*R. Happy are they
who follow the law of the Lord!*

*Point out your rules to me,
and I won't disobey
even one of them.
Help me to understand your Law;
I promise to obey it
with all my heart.*

*R. Happy are they
who follow the law of the Lord!*

SECOND READING

1 Corinthians 2:6–10

God's wisdom predestined our glory before the ages began.

A reading from the first letter of Paul to the Corinthians

Brothers and sisters:
We use wisdom when speaking to people
   who are mature in their faith.
But it is not the wisdom of this world or of its rulers,
who will soon disappear.
We speak of God's hidden and mysterious wisdom
that God decided to use for our glory
   long before the world began.

The rulers of this world
   didn't know anything about this wisdom.
If they had known about it,
they would not have nailed the glorious Lord to a cross.
But it is just as the Scriptures say,
"What God has planned for people who love him
   is more than eyes have seen or ears have heard.
It has never even entered our minds!"

God's Spirit has shown you everything.
His Spirit finds out everything,
even what is deep in the mind of God.

The word of the Lord.

Alleluia

See Matthew 11:25

R. *Alleluia, alleluia.*

*Blessed are you, Father,
Lord of heaven and earth;
you have revealed to little ones
the mysteries of the kingdom.*

R. *Alleluia, alleluia.*

GOSPEL

Matthew 5:23–24

Be reconciled before you offer your gift.

✚ **A reading from the holy gospel according to Matthew**

Jesus said to his disciples:
"If you are about to place your gift on the altar
   and remember that someone is angry with you,
leave your gift there in front of the altar.
Make peace with that person,
then come back and offer your gift to God."

The gospel of the Lord.

SEVENTH SUNDAY IN ORDINARY TIME

FIRST READING

Leviticus 19:1–2, 17–18

You must love your neighbor as yourself.

A reading from the book of Leviticus

The LORD told Moses to say to all of the people of Israel:
Keep yourselves holy.
I am the LORD your God, and I am holy.

Don't secretly hate someone.

Correct anyone who does wrong,
and you won't be guilty of that person's sin.

Don't try to get even.
And don't hold grudges.
You must love others as much as you love yourself.
I am the LORD your God.

The word of the Lord.

Responsorial Psalm R. The Lord is kind and merciful.

Psalm 103:1–2, 3 and 13
(8a)

*With all my heart
I praise the* L ORD ,
*and with all that I am
I praise his holy name!
With all my heart
I praise the* L ORD !
*I will never forget
how kind he has been.*

R. The Lord is kind and merciful.

The L ORD *forgives our sins,
heals us when we are sick.
Just as parents are kind
to their children,
the* L ORD *is kind
to all who worship him.*

R. The Lord is kind and merciful.

SECOND READING

1 Corinthians 3:18–20

Do not fool yourselves.

A reading from the first letter of Paul to the Corinthians

Brothers and sisters:
Don't fool yourselves!
If any of you think you are wise in the things of this world,
 you will have to become foolish
   before you can be truly wise.
This is because God considers the wisdom of this world
   to be foolish.

It is just as the Scriptures say,
"God catches the wise when they try to outsmart him."
The Scriptures also say,
"The Lord knows that the plans made by wise people
   are useless."

The word of the Lord.

Alleluia

1 John 2:5

R. Alleluia, alleluia.

*Whoever keeps the word of Christ,
grows perfect in the love of God.*

R. Alleluia, alleluia.

✠ A reading from the holy gospel according to Matthew

GOSPEL

Matthew 5:38–48

Jesus said to his disciples:
"You know that you have been taught,
'An eye for an eye and a tooth for a tooth.'
But I tell you not to try to get even
    with a person who has done something to you.

"When someone slaps your right cheek,
turn and let that person slap your other cheek.
If someone sues you for your shirt,
give up your coat as well.
If a soldier forces you to carry his pack one mile,
carry it two miles.
When people ask you for something,
give it to them.
When they want to borrow money,
loan it to them.

"You have heard people say,
'Love your neighbors and hate your enemies.'
But I tell you to love your enemies
    and pray for anyone who mistreats you.
Then you will be acting like your Father in heaven.

"He makes the sun rise on both good and bad people.
And he sends rain for the ones who do right
    and for the ones who do wrong.

"If you love only those people who love you,
will God reward you for that?
Even tax collectors love their friends.
If you greet only your friends,
what's so great about that?
Don't even unbelievers do that?
But you must always act like your Father in heaven."

The gospel of the Lord.

Love your enemies.

EIGHTH SUNDAY IN ORDINARY TIME

FIRST READING

A reading from the book of the prophet Isaiah

Isaiah 49:14–15

Even these may forget, says the Lord God; yet I will never forget you.

The people of Jerusalem said,
"The LORD has deserted us and forgotten all about us."

The LORD replied:
"Could a mother forget a child that nurses at her breast
 or fail to love the one who came from her own body?
Even if a mother could forget,
I will never forget you."

The word of the Lord.

Responsorial Psalm

Psalm 62:1-2, 7-8abc
(6a)

R. *Rest in God alone, my soul.*

Only God can save me,
and I calmly wait for him.
God alone is the mighty rock
that keeps me safe
and the fortress
where I feel secure.

R. *Rest in God alone, my soul.*

God saves me and honors me.
He is that mighty rock
where I find safety.
Trust God, my friends,
and always tell him
each one of your concerns.

R. *Rest in God alone, my soul.*

Alleluia　　　　　R. Alleluia, alleluia.

Hebrews 4:12　　　*The word of God is living and active;*
　　　　　　　　　it probes the thoughts and motives
　　　　　　　　　of our heart.

　　　　　　　　　R. Alleluia, alleluia.

GOSPEL　　　✠ **A reading from the holy gospel according to Matthew**

Matthew 6:24–34

Jesus said to his disciples:
"You cannot be the slave of two masters!
You will like one more than the other
　or be more loyal to one than the other.
You cannot serve both God and money.

Do not worry about tomorrow.

"I tell you not to worry about your life.
Don't worry about having something to eat, drink, or wear.
Isn't life more than food or clothing?
Look at the birds in the sky!
They don't plant or harvest.
They don't even store grain in barns.
Yet your Father in heaven takes care of them.
Aren't you worth more than birds?

"Can worry make you live longer?
Why worry about clothes?
Look how the wild flowers grow.
They don't work hard to make their clothes.
But I tell you that Solomon with all his wealth
   was not as well clothed as one of them.
God gives such beauty to everything that grows in the fields,
even though it is here today
   and thrown into a fire tomorrow.
He will surely do even more for you!
Why do you have such little faith?

"Don't worry and ask yourselves,
'Will we have anything to eat?
Will we have anything to drink?
Will we have clothes to wear?'
Only people who don't know God
   are always worrying about such things.
Your Father in heaven knows that you need all of these.
But more than anything else,
put God's work first and do what he wants.
Then all the other things will be yours as well.

"Don't worry about tomorrow.
It will take care of itself.
You have enough to worry about today."

The gospel of the Lord.

NINTH SUNDAY IN ORDINARY TIME

First Reading

A reading from the book of Deuteronomy

Deuteronomy 11:18, 26–28

I set before you today a blessing and a curse.

Moses said to the people:
"Remember these laws and think about them.
Wear them like a sign around your arm
  and on your forehead.

"Today I am giving you the choice of a blessing or a curse.
The Lord your God will bless you,
if you obey the commands that I am giving you today.
But you will be under the Lord's curse,
if you disobey these commands
  and worship gods that are strange to you."

The word of the Lord.

Responsorial Psalm

R. *Lord, be my rock of safety.*

Psalm 31:1 and 2b, 3 and 16 (3b)

*I come to you, LORD,
for protection.
Don't let me be ashamed.
Do as you have promised
and rescue me,
and hurry to save me.*

R. *Lord, be my rock of safety.*

*You, LORD God,
are my mighty rock
and my fortress.
Lead me and guide me,
so that your name
will be honored.
Smile on me, your servant.
Have pity and rescue me.*

R. *Lord, be my rock of safety.*

Alleluia

R. Alleluia, alleluia.

John 15:5

*I am the vine and you are
the branches, says the Lord;
those who live in me, and I in them,
will bear much fruit.*

R. Alleluia, alleluia.

GOSPEL

Matthew 7:21-27

The house built on rock is compared to the house built on sand.

✛ **A reading from the holy gospel according to Matthew**

Jesus said to his disciples:
"Not everyone who calls me their Lord
  will get into the kingdom of heaven.
Only the ones who obey my Father in heaven will get in.
On the day of judgment many will call me their Lord.
They will say, 'We preached in your name,
and in your name we forced out demons
  and worked many miracles.'
But I will tell them,
'I will have nothing to do with you!
Get out of my sight, you evil people!'

"Anyone who hears and obeys these teachings of mine
  is like a wise person who built a house on solid rock.
Rain poured down, rivers flooded,
and winds beat against that house.
But it did not fall,
because it was built on solid rock.

"Anyone who hears my teachings and does not obey them
  is like a foolish person who built a house on sand.
The rain poured down, the rivers flooded,
and the winds blew and beat against that house.
Finally, it fell with a crash."

The gospel of the Lord.

TENTH SUNDAY IN ORDINARY TIME

FIRST READING

A reading from the book of the prophet Hosea

Hosea 6:3–6

Let's try our best to know the LORD.
The coming of the LORD is as certain as the dawn.
He will bless us like showers in winter and spring.

What I want is love, not sacrifice, says the Lord.

People of Judah and Israel,
what must I do with you?
Your love for me is merely a morning cloud or dew
   that quickly disappears.
I sent prophets to you with my message of doom,
and my judgment against you struck like lightning.

When you show mercy and obey me,
it pleases me more than sacrifices and gifts.

The word of the Lord.

Responsorial Psalm

R. To the upright I will show the saving power of God.

Psalm 50:8–9, 14–15 (23b)

Although you offer sacrifices and always bring gifts, I won't accept your offerings of bulls and goats.

R. To the upright I will show the saving power of God.

I am God Most High! The only sacrifice I want is for you to be thankful and to keep your word. Pray to me in time of trouble. I will rescue you, and you will honor me.

R. To the upright I will show the saving power of God.

SECOND READING

Romans 4:18–21

Abraham drew strength from his faith while giving glory to God.

A reading from the letter of Paul to the Romans

Brothers and sisters:
God promised Abraham a lot of descendants.
And when it all seemed hopeless,
Abraham still had faith in God
  and became the ancestor of many nations.

Abraham's faith never became weak,
not even when he was nearly a hundred years old.
He knew that he was almost dead
  and that his wife Sarah could not have children.
But Abraham never doubted or questioned God's promise.
His faith made him strong,
and he gave all the credit to God.

Abraham was certain that God could do
  what he had promised.

The word of the Lord.

Alleluia

Luke 4:18

R. *Alleluia, alleluia.*

The Lord sent me to bring
good news to the poor
and freedom to prisoners.

R. *Alleluia, alleluia.*

GOSPEL

Matthew 9:9–13

✢ A reading from the holy gospel according to Matthew

As Jesus was leaving Capernaum,
he saw a tax collector named Matthew
   sitting at the place for paying taxes.
Jesus said to him, "Come with me."
Matthew got up and went with him.

Later, Jesus and his disciples
   were having dinner at Matthew's house.
Many tax collectors and other sinners were also there.
Some Pharisees asked Jesus' disciples,
"Why does your teacher eat with tax collectors
   and other sinners?"

Jesus heard them and answered,
"Healthy people don't need a doctor,
but sick people do.
Go and learn what the Scriptures mean when they say,
'Instead of offering sacrifices to me,
I want you to be merciful to others.'
I didn't come to invite good people to be my followers.
I came to invite sinners."

The gospel of the Lord.

I did not come to call the just, but sinners.

ELEVENTH SUNDAY IN ORDINARY TIME

First Reading

A reading from the book of Exodus

Exodus 19:1–6a

You will be a kingdom of priests, a consecrated nation.

The people of Israel left Rephidim.
And two months after leaving Egypt,
they reached the desert near Mount Sinai.
They set up camp there at the foot of the mountain.

Moses went up the mountain to meet with the Lord God,
who told him to say to the people:

"You saw what I, the Lord, did in Egypt.
You know how like a mighty eagle
I brought you here to me.
Now if you will obey me and are faithful to me,
you will be my people.
The whole world is mine.
But you will be mine in a special way
  and serve me as priests."

The word of the Lord.

Responsorial Psalm

R. We are his people:
the sheep of his flock.

Psalm 100:1–2, 3, 5
(3c)

Shout praises to the LORD,
everyone on this earth.
Be joyful and sing
as you come in
to worship the LORD!

R. We are his people:
the sheep of his flock.

You know the LORD is God!
He created us,
and we belong to him;
we are his people,
the sheep in his pasture.

R. We are his people:
the sheep of his flock.

The LORD is good!
His love and faithfulness
will last forever.

R. We are his people:
the sheep of his flock.

Second Reading

Romans 5:6–11

We have been reconciled to God through the death of his Son; we are saved by his life.

A reading from the letter of Paul to the Romans

Brothers and sisters:
Christ died for us at a time
　　when we were helpless and sinful.
No one is really willing to die for an honest person,
though someone might be willing to die
　　for a truly good person.
But God showed how much he loved us
by having Christ die for us,
even though we were sinful.

But there is more!
Now that God has accepted us
　　because Christ sacrificed his life's blood,
we will also be kept safe from God's anger.
Even when we were still God's enemies,
he made peace with us,
because his Son died for us.
Yet something even greater than friendship is ours.
Now that we are at peace with God,
we will be saved by his Son's life.

And in addition to everything else,
we are happy because God sent our Lord Jesus Christ
　　to make peace with us.

The word of the Lord.

Alleluia　　　　　　　R. Alleluia, alleluia.

Mark 1:15　　　　　　　*The kingdom of God is near;*
　　　　　　　　　　　　repent and believe the good news!

　　　　　　　　　　　　R. *Alleluia, alleluia.*

ELEVENTH SUNDAY IN ORDINARY TIME

GOSPEL

Matthew 9:36—10:8

✠ A reading from the holy gospel according to Matthew

When Jesus saw the crowds,
he felt sorry for them.
They were confused and helpless,
like sheep without a shepherd.

He said to his disciples,
"A large crop is in the fields,
but there are only a few workers.
Ask the Lord in charge of the harvest
   to send out workers to bring it in."

Jesus summoned his twelve disciples, and sent them out.

Jesus called together his twelve disciples.
He gave them the power to force out evil spirits
   and to heal every kind of disease and sickness.

The first of the twelve apostles was Simon,
better known as Peter.
His brother Andrew was an apostle,
and so were James and John, the two sons of Zebedee.
Philip, Bartholomew, Thomas,
   Matthew the tax collector, James the son of Alphaeus,
   and Thaddaeus were also apostles.
The others were Simon, known as the Eager One,
   and Judas Iscariot, who later betrayed Jesus.

Jesus sent out the twelve apostles with these instructions:
"Stay away from the Gentiles
and don't go to any Samaritan town.
Go only to the people of Israel,
because they are like a flock of lost sheep.

"As you go,
announce that the kingdom of heaven will soon be here.
Heal the sick, raise the dead to life,
heal people who have leprosy,
and force out demons.
You received without paying,
now give without being paid."

The gospel of the Lord.

TWELFTH SUNDAY IN ORDINARY TIME

FIRST READING

A reading from the book of the prophet Jeremiah

Jeremiah 20:10–12a, 13

I heard the crowds whisper, "Everyone's afraid!
Tell on him! Tell on him!"
All of my friends are waiting for me to make a mistake.
They say, "He will slip up.
Then we can trap him and get even at last."

The Lord has delivered the soul of the needy from the hands of those who are evil.

But the LORD is with me like a mighty soldier.
And those troublemakers will stumble,
   then fall down and fail.
They will be forever disgraced and terribly ashamed.

LORD All-Powerful, you test everyone who does right,
and you know everything anyone thinks or feels.

Sing and praise the LORD!
He rescues the helpless from cruel oppressors.

The word of the Lord.

Responsorial Psalm R. Lord, in your great love, answer me.

I pray to you, Lord.
So when the time is right,
answer me and help me
Psalm 69:13, 16, 29b–30a *with your wonderful love.*
(14c)

R. *Lord, in your great love, answer me.*

Answer me, Lord!
You are kind and good.
Pay attention to me!
You are truly merciful.

R. *Lord, in your great love, answer me.*

Protect me, God,
and keep me safe!
I will praise the Lord God
with a song.

R. *Lord, in your great love, answer me.*

Alleluia R. *Alleluia, alleluia.*

John 15:26b, 27a

*The Spirit of truth will bear witness to me, says the Lord,
and you also will be my witnesses.*

R. *Alleluia, alleluia.*

GOSPEL ✢ **A reading from the holy gospel according to Matthew**

Matthew 10:26–31

Jesus said to his disciples:
"Don't be afraid of anyone!
Everything that is hidden will be found out,
and every secret will be known.

"Whatever I say to you in the dark,
you must tell in the light.
And you must announce from the housetops
   whatever I have whispered to you.

Do not fear those who can kill the body.

"Don't be afraid of people.
They can kill you,
but they cannot harm your soul.
Instead, you should fear God
who can destroy both your body and your soul in hell.

"Aren't two sparrows sold for only a penny?
But your Father knows when any one of them
   falls to the ground.
Even the hairs on your head are counted.
So don't be afraid!
You are worth much more than many sparrows."

The gospel of the Lord.

THIRTEENTH SUNDAY IN ORDINARY TIME

First Reading

A reading from the second book of Kings

2 Kings 4:8–11, 14–16a

That is the holy man of God; let him remain there.

One day Elisha went to the town of Shunem.
A rich woman lived there,
and she invited him for a meal.
Each time Elisha was in town after that,
he would eat at her home.

The woman said to her husband,
"I'm sure that this man who comes by here so often
    is a holy man of God.
Let's build him a small room on our flat roof.
We can put a bed, a table, a chair,
    and an oil lamp in the room.
He can stay there whenever he comes to visit us."
The next time Elisha came to Shunem,
he spent the night in his room.

Elisha asked his servant Gehazi,
"What can we do to repay this woman for being so kind?"

Gehazi answered,
"She doesn't have a son, and her husband is old."

Elisha said to Gehazi,
"Tell the woman to come here."
He told her,
and she came and stood in the doorway of the room.

Elisha promised the woman,
"Next year about this time you will have a son of your own."

The word of the Lord.

Responsorial Psalm

R. For ever I will sing
the goodness of the Lord.

Psalm 89:1–2, 15–16
(2a)

Our LORD, I will sing
of your love forever.
Everyone yet to be born
will hear me praise
your faithfulness.
I will tell them, "God's love
can always be trusted,
and his faithfulness lasts
as long as the heavens."

R. For ever I will sing
the goodness of the Lord.

Our LORD, you bless those
who join in the festival
and walk in the brightness
of your presence.
We are happy all day
because of you,
and your saving power
brings honor to us.

R. For ever I will sing
the goodness of the Lord.

SECOND READING

Romans 6:3–4, 8–9

Buried with Christ in baptism, we shall walk in the newness of life.

A reading from the letter of Paul to the Romans

Brothers and sisters:
Don't you know that all who share in Christ Jesus
  by being baptized also share in his death?
When we were baptized,
we died and were buried with Christ.
We were baptized, so that we would live a new life,
as Christ was raised to life by the glory of God the Father.

As surely as we died with Christ,
we believe we will also live with him.
We know that death no longer has any power over Christ.
He died and was raised to life,
never again to die.

The word of the Lord.

Alleluia

1 Peter 2:9

R. *Alleluia, alleluia.*

You are a chosen race,
a royal priesthood, a holy people.
Praise God who called you
out of darkness
and into his marvelous light.

R. *Alleluia, alleluia.*

✠ A reading from the holy gospel according to Matthew

Jesus said to his disciples:
"Anyone who welcomes you welcomes me.
And anyone who welcomes me
　also welcomes the one who sent me.

"Anyone who welcomes a prophet,
　just because that person is a prophet,
　will be given the same reward as a prophet.
Anyone who welcomes a good person,
　just because that person is good,
　will be given the same reward as a good person.

"And anyone who gives one of my most humble followers
　a cup of cool water,
　just because that person is my follower,
　will surely be rewarded."

The gospel of the Lord.

GOSPEL

Matthew 10:40–42

Anyone who welcomes you, welcomes me.

FOURTEENTH SUNDAY IN ORDINARY TIME

FIRST READING

A reading from the book of the prophet Zechariah

Zechariah 9:9–10

The LORD says this:
Everyone in Jerusalem, celebrate and rejoice.
Your king has won the victory,
and he is coming to you.
He is humble and rides on a donkey.
He comes on the colt of a donkey.

See how humbly your king comes to you!

I, the LORD, will take away all war chariots and horses
    from Israel and Jerusalem.
Bows that were made for battle will be destroyed.

I will bring peace to nations,
and your king will rule from sea to sea.
His kingdom will reach from the Euphrates River
    across all the earth.

The word of the Lord.

Responsorial Psalm

R. *I will praise your name for ever,*
my king and my God.
or:
R. *Alleluia.*

Psalm 145:1–2, 8–9, 13cd–14
(see 1)

I will praise you,
my God and King,
and always honor your name.
I will praise you each day
and always honor your name.

R. *I will praise your name for ever,*
my king and my God.
or:
R. *Alleluia.*

You are merciful, LORD!
You are kind and patient
and always loving.
You are good to everyone,
and you take care
of all your creation.

R. *I will praise your name for ever,*
my king and my God.
or:
R. *Alleluia.*

Our LORD, you keep your word
and do everything you say.
When someone stumbles or falls,
you give a helping hand.

R. *I will praise your name for ever,*
my king and my God.
or:
R. *Alleluia.*

Second Reading

Romans 8:9, 11

God's Spirit now lives in you.

A reading from the letter of Paul to the Romans

Brothers and sisters:
You are no longer ruled by your desires,
but by God's Spirit, who lives in you.
People who don't have the Spirit of Christ in them
    don't belong to him.

God raised Jesus to life!
God's Spirit now lives in you,
and he will raise you to life by his Spirit.

The word of the Lord.

Alleluia

See Matthew 11:25

R. Alleluia, alleluia.

*Blessed are you, Father,
Lord of heaven and earth;
you have revealed to little ones
the mysteries of the kingdom.*

R. Alleluia, alleluia.

Gospel

✚ **A reading from the holy gospel according to Matthew**

Matthew 11:25–30

On one occasion Jesus said:
"My Father, Lord of heaven and earth,
I am glad that you hid all this from wise and educated people
    and showed it to ordinary people.
Yes, Father, that is what pleased you.

"My Father has given me everything,
and he is the only one who knows the Son.
The only one who truly knows the Father is the Son.
But the Son wants to tell others about the Father,
so that they can know him too.

"If you are tired from carrying heavy burdens,
come to me and I will give you rest.
Take the yoke I give you.
Put it on your shoulders and learn from me.
I am gentle and humble,
and you will find rest.
This yoke is easy to bear,
and this burden is light."

The gospel of the Lord.

*I am gentle
and humble of heart.*

FIFTEENTH SUNDAY IN ORDINARY TIME

FIRST READING

A reading from the book of the prophet Isaiah

Isaiah 55:10–11

The rain makes the earth fruitful.

The rain and the snow fall from the sky.
But they don't return without watering the earth
   that produces seeds to plant and grain to eat.
And that's how it is with my words.
They don't return to me
   without doing everything I sent them to do.

The word of the Lord.

Responsorial Psalm

R. *The seed that falls on good ground
will yield a fruitful harvest.*

Psalm 65:9, 11–12, 13
(Luke 8:8)

*Our God, you take care of the earth
and send rain to help the soil
grow all kinds of crops.
Your rivers never run dry,
and you prepare the earth
to produce much grain.*

R. *The seed that falls on good ground
will yield a fruitful harvest.*

*Wherever your footsteps
touch the earth,
a rich harvest is gathered.
Desert pastures blossom,
and mountains celebrate.*

R. *The seed that falls on good ground
will yield a fruitful harvest.*

*Meadows are filled
with sheep and goats;
valleys overflow with grain
and echo with joyful songs.*

R. *The seed that falls on good ground
will yield a fruitful harvest.*

Second Reading

Romans 8:14–18

God's Spirit leads us to share in the glory of Christ.

A reading from the letter of Paul to the Romans

Brothers and sisters:
Only those people who are led by God's Spirit
    are his children.
God's Spirit doesn't make us slaves who are afraid of him.
Instead, we become his children and call him our Father.
God's Spirit makes us sure that we are his children.

His Spirit lets us know that together with Christ
    we will be given what God has promised.
We will also share in the glory of Christ,
because we have suffered with him.

I am sure that what we are suffering now
    cannot compare with the glory that will be shown to us.

The word of the Lord.

Alleluia

R. Alleluia, alleluia.

*The seed is the word of God,
Christ is the sower;
all who come to him will live for ever.*

R. Alleluia, alleluia.

Gospel

✠ A reading from the holy gospel according to Matthew

Matthew 13:1–9

Jesus went out beside Lake Galilee,
where he sat down to teach.
Such large crowds gathered around him
   that he had to sit in a boat,
while the people stood on the shore.
Then he taught them many things by using stories.

He said: "A farmer went out to scatter seed in a field.
While the farmer was scattering the seed,
some of it fell along the road and was eaten by birds.
Other seeds fell on thin, rocky ground
   and quickly started growing
because the soil was not very deep.
But when the sun came up,
the plants were scorched and dried up,
because they did not have enough roots.

A sower went out to sow.

"Some other seeds fell where thorn bushes grew up
   and choked the plants.
But a few seeds did fall on good ground
where the plants produced a hundred or sixty
   or thirty times as much as was scattered.
"If you have ears, pay attention!"

The gospel of the Lord.

SIXTEENTH SUNDAY IN ORDINARY TIME

FIRST READING

A reading from the book of Wisdom

Wisdom 12:13, 16–19

There is no God but you,
and you care for all of us.
You don't have to prove that you judge fairly.

Your strength gives you the power to do right,
and because you rule over all,
you have pity on everyone.

In place of sin you give repentance.

When someone doubts how strong you are,
you show your strength.
And you correct everyone who is too proud.

You are a powerful Master.
But you judge us with kindness and rule with great mercy,
because you have the power to do whatever you want.

By doing such things,
you have taught your people
that those who do right must also care about others.
And you have given your children a wonderful hope
 by helping them turn from sin.

The word of the Lord.

Responsorial Psalm R. *Lord, you are good and forgiving.*

*You willingly forgive,
and your love is always there
for those who pray to you.*

Psalm 86:5–6, 15–16de
(5a)

*Please listen, LORD!
Answer my prayer for help.*

R. *Lord, you are good and forgiving.*

*You, the Lord God,
are kind and merciful.
You don't easily get angry,
and your love
can always be trusted.
Look on me with kindness.
Make me strong and save me.*

R. *Lord, you are good and forgiving.*

Second Reading

Romans 8:26–27

That very Spirit intercedes for us with longings too deep for words.

A reading from the letter of Paul to the Romans

Brothers and sisters:
In certain ways we are weak,
    but the Spirit is here to help us.
For example, when we don't know what to pray for,
the Spirit prays for us in ways that cannot be put into words.
All of our thoughts are known to God.
He can understand what is in the mind of the Spirit,
as the Spirit prays for God's people.

The word of the Lord.

Alleluia

See Matthew 11:25

R. Alleluia, alleluia.

*Blessed are you, Father,
Lord of heaven and earth;
you have revealed to little ones
the mysteries of the kingdom.*

R. Alleluia, alleluia.

SIXTEENTH SUNDAY IN ORDINARY TIME

✚ A reading from the holy gospel according to Matthew

GOSPEL

Jesus told his disciples this story:

Matthew 13:24–30

"The kingdom of heaven is like what happened
   when a farmer scattered good seed in a field.
But while everyone was sleeping,
an enemy came and scattered weed seeds in the field
   and then left.
When the plants came up and began to ripen,
the farmer's servants could see the weeds.

Let them grow together until the harvest.

"The servants came and asked,
'Sir, didn't you scatter good seed in your field?
Where did these weeds come from?'
'An enemy did this,' he replied.

"His servants then asked,
'Do you want us to go out and pull up the weeds?'
'No!' he answered.
'You might also pull up the wheat.
Leave the weeds alone until harvest time.
Then I'll tell my workers to gather the weeds
and tie them up and burn them.
But I'll have them store the wheat in my barn.'"

The gospel of the Lord.

SEVENTEENTH SUNDAY IN ORDINARY TIME

First Reading

1 Kings 3:5, 7–12

You have asked for wisdom.

A reading from the first book of Kings

One night at Gibeon,
  God appeared to Solomon in a dream and said,
"Ask me for anything you want."

Solomon answered,
"My Lord and God, I am your servant.
You have made me king in place of my father David.
But I don't know any more about being king
  than a child would know.
And I must serve your chosen people,
even though they are a great nation
  with more people than can be counted.
Please make me wise enough to rule them well
  and know the difference between right and wrong.
No one is really able to rule this great nation of yours."

The Lord was pleased that Solomon had asked this,
  and he said:
"I will answer your prayer.
You will be wise and know more
  than anyone who has ever lived or ever will live.
You didn't ask to live a long time or to be rich,
and you didn't ask for your enemies to be destroyed.
All you wanted was to be honest and fair."

The word of the Lord.

Responsorial Psalm

Psalm 119:57 and 72, 127–128 (97a)

R. *Lord, I love your commands.*

*You, LORD, are my choice,
and I will obey you.
I would rather obey you
than to have a thousand pieces
of silver and gold.*

R. *Lord, I love your commands.*

*Your laws mean more to me
than the finest gold.
I follow all of your commands,
but I hate anyone
who leads me astray.*

R. *Lord, I love your commands.*

Second Reading

Romans 8:28–30

God predestined us to become true images of his Son.

A reading from the letter of Paul to the Romans

Brothers and sisters:
We know that God is always at work
   for the good of everyone who loves him.
They are the ones God has chosen for his purpose,
and he has always known who his chosen ones would be.
He had decided to let them become like his own Son,
so that his Son would be the first of many children.
God then accepted the people
   he had already decided to choose,
and he has shared his glory with them.

The word of the Lord.

Alleluia

See Matthew 11:25

R. *Alleluia, alleluia.*

Blessed are you, Father,
Lord of heaven and earth;
you have revealed to little ones
the mysteries of the kingdom.

R. *Alleluia, alleluia.*

✢ A reading from the holy gospel according to Matthew

Jesus said to his disciples:
"The kingdom of heaven is like what happens
   when someone finds treasure hidden in a field
   and buries it again.
A person like that is happy and goes and sells everything
   in order to buy that field.

"The kingdom of heaven is like what happens
   when a shop owner is looking for fine pearls.
After finding a very valuable one,
the owner goes and sells everything
   in order to buy that pearl."

The gospel of the Lord.

GOSPEL

Matthew 13:44–46

He sold all that he had and bought the field.

EIGHTEENTH SUNDAY IN ORDINARY TIME

First Reading

A reading from the book of the prophet Isaiah

Isaiah 55:1–3

T he L ORD says this:
If you are thirsty,
come and drink water!
If you don't have any money,
buy food and eat it.
Come and buy wine and milk

Hasten and eat. without paying a cent.
Why waste your money
on something less than food?
Why work hard for something
that doesn't satisfy?
Listen carefully to me,
and you will enjoy
the very best foods.
Listen carefully! Come to me,
and you will live.
I will promise you
the eternal love and loyalty
that I promised David.

The word of the Lord.

Responsorial Psalm

R. *You open your hand to feed us, Lord;*
you answer all our needs.

Psalm 145:8–9, 15–16
(see 16)

You are merciful, LORD!
You are kind and patient
and always loving.
You are good to everyone,
and you take care
of all your creation.

R. *You open your hand to feed us, Lord;*
you answer all our needs.

Everyone depends on you,
and when the time is right,
you provide them with food.
By your own hand you satisfy
the desires of all who live.

R. *You open your hand to feed us, Lord;*
you answer all our needs.

SECOND READING

Romans 8:35, 37–39

Nothing can come between us and the love of God made visible in Christ Jesus our Lord.

A reading from the letter of Paul to the Romans

Brothers and sisters:
Can anything separate us from the love of Christ?
Can trouble, suffering, and hard times,
   or hunger and nakedness, or danger and death?

In everything we have won more than a victory
because of Christ who loves us.

I am sure that nothing can separate us from God's love—
   not life or death, not angels or spirits,
   not the present or the future,
   and not powers above or powers below.
Nothing in all creation can separate us
   from God's love for us in Christ Jesus our Lord!

The word of the Lord.

Alleluia

Matthew 4:4b

R. *Alleluia, alleluia.*

*No one lives on bread alone,
but on every word that comes
from the mouth of God.*

R. *Alleluia, alleluia.*

GOSPEL

Matthew 14:13–21

✢ **A reading from the holy gospel according to Matthew**

After Jesus heard about John,
he crossed Lake Galilee to go to some place
   where he could be alone.
But the crowds found out
   and followed him on foot from the towns.
When Jesus got out of the boat, he saw the large crowd.
He felt sorry for them and healed everyone who was sick.

That evening the disciples came to Jesus and said,
"This place is like a desert, and it is already late.
Let the crowds leave,
so they can go to the villages and buy some food."

Jesus replied, "They don't have to leave.
Why don't you give them something to eat?"
But they said, "We have only five small loaves of bread
   and two fish."

Jesus asked his disciples to bring the food to him,
and he told the crowd to sit down on the grass.
Jesus took the five loaves and the two fish.
He looked up toward heaven and blessed the food.
Then he broke the bread and handed it to his disciples,
and they gave it to the people.

After everyone had eaten all they wanted,
Jesus' disciples picked up twelve large baskets of leftovers.
There were about five thousand men who ate,
   not counting the women and children.

The gospel of the Lord.

They all ate and were satisfied.

NINETEENTH SUNDAY IN ORDINARY TIME

First Reading

1 Kings 19:9a, 11–13a

*Go out and stand
on the mountain
before the Lord God.*

A reading from the first book of Kings

Elijah went into a cave and spent the night.

The Lord said, "Elijah, go out and stand on the mountain.
I am going to pass that way."

At once a strong and mighty wind shook the mountain
    and shattered the rocks.
But the Lord was not in the wind.

An earthquake shook the ground,
but the Lord was not in the earthquake.
After the earthquake there was a fire,
but the Lord was not in the fire.

After the fire,
hardly a sound was heard.
Elijah covered his face with his robe
    and went out and stood at the entrance to the cave.

The word of the Lord.

Responsorial Psalm

Psalm 85:8abc and 9,
10–11, 12–13
(8)

R. Lord, show us your mercy and love,
and grant us your salvation.

I will listen to you, LORD God,
because you promise peace
to those who are faithful.
You are ready to rescue
everyone who worships you,
so that you will live with us
in all of your glory.

R. Lord, show us your mercy and love,
and grant us your salvation.

Love and loyalty
will come together;
goodness and peace will unite.
Loyalty will sprout
from the ground;
justice will look down
from the sky above.

R. Lord, show us your mercy and love,
and grant us your salvation.

Our LORD, you will bless us;
our land will produce
wonderful crops.
Justice will march in front,
making a path
for you to follow.

R. Lord, show us your mercy and love,
and grant us your salvation.

Alleluia R. *Alleluia, alleluia.*

See Psalm 130:5 *I hope in the Lord,*
I trust in his word.

R. *Alleluia, alleluia.*

GOSPEL ✢ **A reading from the holy gospel according to Matthew**

Matthew 14:22–33

Jesus made his disciples get into a boat
   and start back across the lake.
But he stayed until he had sent the crowds away.
Then he went up on a mountain
   where he could be alone and pray.
Later that evening, he was still there.

Command me to come to you over the water.

By this time the boat was a long way from the shore.
It was going against the wind
   and was being tossed around by the waves.
A little while before morning,
Jesus came walking on the water toward his disciples.
When they saw him, they thought he was a ghost.
They were terrified and started screaming.

At once Jesus said to them, "Don't worry!
I am Jesus. Don't be afraid."

Peter replied, "Lord, if it is really you,
tell me to come to you on the water."

"Come on!" Jesus said.
Peter then got out of the boat
   and started walking on the water toward him.

But when Peter saw how strong the wind was,
he was afraid and started sinking.

"Lord, save me!" he shouted.

Right away Jesus reached out his hand.
He helped Peter up and said,
"You surely don't have much faith.
Why do you doubt?"

When Jesus and Peter got into the boat, the wind died down.
The men in the boat worshiped Jesus and said,
"You really are the Son of God!"

The gospel of the Lord.

TWENTIETH SUNDAY IN ORDINARY TIME

FIRST READING | **A reading from the book of the prophet Isaiah**

Isaiah 56:1, 6–7

The LORD said,
"Be honest and fair!

"Soon I will come to save you,
and my saving power will be seen.
Foreigners will follow me.

I will lead the foreigners to my holy mountain.

They will love me and worship in my name.
They will respect the Sabbath and keep our agreement.

"Then I will bring them to my holy mountain
   and let them celebrate in my house of worship.
Their sacrifices and offerings
   will all be welcome on my altar.
And my house will be known
   as a house of worship for all nations."

The word of the Lord.

Responsorial Psalm   R. *O God, let all the nations praise you!*

Our God, be kind and bless us!
Be pleased and smile.
Then everyone on earth
will learn to follow you,
and all nations will see
your power to save us.

Psalm 67:1–2, 4, 5 and 7
(4)

R. *O God, let all the nations praise you!*

Let the nations celebrate
with joyful songs,
because you judge fairly
and guide all nations.

R. *O God, let all the nations praise you!*

Make everyone praise you
and shout your praises.
Pray for his blessings to continue
and for everyone on earth
to worship our God.

R. *O God, let all the nations praise you!*

Alleluia

See Matthew 4:23

R. *Alleluia, alleluia.*

*Jesus preached the good news
of the kingdom
and healed all who were sick.*

R. *Alleluia, alleluia.*

GOSPEL

Matthew 15:21–28

Woman, your faith is great.

✠ **A reading from the holy gospel according to Matthew**

Jesus went to the territory near the cities of Tyre and Sidon.
Suddenly a Canaanite woman from there came out shouting,
"Lord and Son of David, have pity on me!
My daughter is full of demons."

Jesus did not say a word.
But the woman kept following along and shouting,
so his disciples came up and asked him to send her away.

Jesus said, "I was sent only to the people of Israel!
They are like a flock of lost sheep."

The woman came closer.
Then she kneeled down and begged,
"Lord, please help me!"

Jesus replied,
"It isn't right to take food away from children
   and feed it to dogs."

"Lord, that's true," the woman said,
"but even dogs get the crumbs
   that fall from their owner's table."

Jesus answered,
   "Dear woman, you really do have a lot of faith,
and you will be given what you want."

At that moment her daughter was healed.

The gospel of the Lord.

TWENTY-FIRST SUNDAY IN ORDINARY TIME

FIRST READING

Romans 11:33–36

From Christ, through him, and in him are all things.

A reading from the letter of Paul to the Romans

Brothers and sisters:
Who can measure the wealth and wisdom
   and knowledge of God?
Who can understand his decisions or explain what he does?

  "Has anyone ever known the thoughts of the Lord
   or given him advice?
  Has anyone loaned something to the Lord
   that must be repaid?"

Everything comes from the Lord.
All things were made because of him and will return to him.
Praise the Lord forever! Amen.

The word of the Lord.

Responsorial Psalm R. Lord, your love is eternal.

With all my heart
I praise you, LORD.
In the presence of angels
I sing your praises.
I worship at your holy temple.

Psalm 138:1–2a, 2bc and 3, 6 and 8cde (8b)

R. Lord, your love is eternal.

I praise you for your love
and your faithfulness.
When I asked for your help,
you answered my prayer
and gave me courage.

R. Lord, your love is eternal.

Though you are above us all,
you care for humble people,
and you keep a close watch
on everyone who is proud.
Your love never fails.
You have made us what we are.
Don't give up on us now!

R. Lord, your love is eternal.

TWENTY-FIRST SUNDAY IN ORDINARY TIME

Alleluia R. *Alleluia, alleluia.*

Matthew 16:18 *You are Peter, the rock on which*
I will build my Church;
the gates of hell
will not prevail against it.

R. *Alleluia, alleluia.*

GOSPEL ✚ **A reading from the holy gospel according to Matthew**

Matthew 16:13–20
When Jesus and his disciples
   were near the town of Caesarea Philippi,
he asked them, "What do people say about the Son of Man?"

The disciples answered, "Some people say you are John the Baptist
   or maybe Elijah or Jeremiah or some other prophet."

You are Peter;
to you I will give the keys
of the kingdom of heaven.

Then Jesus asked them, "But who do you say I am?"

Simon Peter spoke up,
"You are the Messiah, the Son of the living God."

Jesus told him:
"Simon, son of Jonah, you are blessed!
You didn't discover this on your own.
It was shown to you by my Father in heaven.
So I will call you Peter, which means 'a rock.'
On this rock I will build my Church,
and death itself will not have any power over it.
I will give you the keys to the kingdom of heaven,
and God in heaven will allow whatever you allow on earth.
But he will not allow anything that you don't allow."

Jesus told his disciples not to tell anyone
   that he was the Messiah.

The gospel of the Lord.

TWENTY-SECOND SUNDAY IN ORDINARY TIME

FIRST READING

Jeremiah 20:7–9

The word of the Lord God has meant derision for me.

A reading from the book of the prophet Jeremiah

Jeremiah spoke to the Lord and said:
"You tricked me, Lord, and I was really fooled.
With your mighty power you defeated me.

"No one ever stops sneering or telling jokes about me.
All I can say to anyone is, 'Death and destruction!'

"Your message has brought me insults and abuse.
Sometimes I say to myself,
'I won't think about you or mention your name.'
But your message is like a fire burning inside me,
and I can't keep quiet."

The word of the Lord.

Responsorial Psalm

R. My soul is thirsting for you,
O Lord my God.

You are my God. I worship you.
In my heart, I long for you,
as I would long for a stream.

Psalm 63:1abc, 2–3, 4–5
(2b)

R. My soul is thirsting for you,
O Lord my God.

I have seen your power
and your glory
in the place of worship.
Your love means more
than life to me,
and I praise you.

R. My soul is thirsting for you,
O Lord my God.

As long as I live,
I will pray to you.
I will sing joyful praises
and be filled with excitement
like a guest at a banquet.

R. My soul is thirsting for you,
O Lord my God.

SECOND READING

Romans 12:1-2

Offer your bodies as a living, holy sacrifice.

A reading from the letter of Paul to the Romans

Dear friends, God is good.
So I beg you to offer your bodies to him
    as a living sacrifice, pure and pleasing.
That's the most sensible way to serve God.

Don't be like the people of this world,
but let God change the way you think.
Then you will know
    how to do everything that is good and pleasing to him.

The word of the Lord.

Alleluia

See Ephesians 1:17-18

R. *Alleluia, alleluia.*

May the Father
of our Lord Jesus Christ
enlighten the eyes of our heart,
that we might see
how great is the hope
to which we are called.

R. *Alleluia, alleluia.*

✚ A reading from the holy gospel according to Matthew

GOSPEL

Jesus began telling his disciples what would happen to him.
He said, "I must go to Jerusalem.
There the nation's leaders, the chief priests,
and the teachers of the Law of Moses
    will make me suffer terribly.
I will be killed,
but three days later I will rise to life."

Matthew 16:21–25

Peter took Jesus aside and told him to stop talking like that.
He said, "Lord, surely God won't let this happen to you!"

All who wish to follow me must deny themselves.

Jesus turned to Peter and said, "Satan, get away from me!
You're in my way because you think like everyone else
    and not like God."

Then Jesus said to his disciples:
"If any of you want to be my followers,
you must forget about yourself.
You must take up your cross and follow me.
If you want to save your life,
you will destroy it.

"But if you give up your life for me,
you will find it."

The gospel of the Lord.

TWENTY-THIRD SUNDAY IN ORDINARY TIME

FIRST READING

A reading from the book of the prophet Ezekiel

Ezekiel 33:7–9

The Lord said:
"Ezekiel, you are a mere human,
but I have chosen you to be a watchman
   for the people of Israel.
So listen to what I say
and then warn them for me.

If you have not warned the wicked, then I will hold you responsible for their death.

"When I tell evil people that they will die
   because of their sins,
you must try to make them turn from their evil ways.
If you don't warn them,
you are responsible for what happens to them.
If you do warn them to turn from their evil ways,
   and they don't,
then they will die.
But you won't be responsible."

The word of the Lord.

Responsorial Psalm

R. *If today you hear God's voice,
harden not your hearts.*

Sing joyful songs to the LORD!
*Praise the mighty rock
where we are safe.
Come to worship him
with thankful hearts
and songs of praise.*

Psalm 95:1–2, 6–7abcd, 7e–9
(8)

R. *If today you hear God's voice,
harden not your hearts.*

*Bow down and worship
the* LORD *our Creator!
The* LORD *is our God,
and we are his people,
the sheep he takes care of
in his own pasture.*

R. *If today you hear God's voice,
harden not your hearts.*

*Listen to God's voice today!
Don't be stubborn and rebel
as your ancestors did
at Meribah and at Massah
out in the desert.
For forty years
they tested God and saw
the things he did.*

R. *If today you hear God's voice,
harden not your hearts.*

TWENTY-THIRD SUNDAY IN ORDINARY TIME

SECOND READING

Romans 13:8–10

Love is the fulfillment of the law.

A reading from the letter of Paul to the Romans

Brothers and sisters:
Let love be your only debt!
If you love others,
you have done all that the Law demands.

In the Law there are many commands, such as,

"Be faithful in marriage.
Do not murder. Do not steal.
Do not want what belongs to others."

But all of these are summed up in the command that says,
"Love others as much as you love yourself."
No one who loves others will harm them.

So love is all that the Law demands.

The word of the Lord.

Alleluia

2 Corinthians 5:19

R. *Alleluia, alleluia.*

*God was in Christ,
to reconcile the world to himself;
and the good news of reconciliation
he has entrusted to us.*

R. *Alleluia, alleluia.*

GOSPEL

Matthew 18:15–17

✚ A reading from the holy gospel according to Matthew

Jesus said to his disciples:
"If one of my followers sins against you,
go and point out what was wrong.
But do it in private,
just between the two of you.
If that person listens,
you have won back a follower.
But if that one refuses to listen,
take along one or two others.

"The Scriptures teach that every complaint
    must be proven true by two or more witnesses.
If the follower refuses to listen to them,
report the matter to the church.

"Anyone who refuses to listen to the church
    must be treated like an unbeliever or a tax collector."

The gospel of the Lord.

If your brother or sister listens to you, you will have won that person back.

TWENTY-FOURTH SUNDAY IN ORDINARY TIME

FIRST READING

Sirach 28:2–5, 6b–7

Forgive your neighbor's faults, and when you pray, your sins will be forgiven.

A reading from the book of Sirach

If you forgive your friends when they mistreat you,
your prayers will be answered and your sins forgiven.
If you stay angry with someone,
don't expect the Lord to heal you.
Don't ask God to forgive you,
if you don't have pity on others.
God won't forgive you,
if you stay angry at someone.

So stop holding grudges and start obeying God.
Think about the commands and the promise
   of God Most High.
Then forget about the sins and the ignorance of others.

The word of the Lord.

Responsorial Psalm R. The Lord is kind and merciful.

*With all my heart
I praise the L*ORD*,
and with all that I am
I praise his holy name!
With all my heart
I praise the L*ORD*!
I will never forget
how kind he has been.*

Psalm 103:1–2, 3–4, 11–12
(8a)

R. *The Lord is kind and merciful.*

*The L*ORD *forgives our sins,
heals us when we are sick,
and protects us from death.
His kindness and love
are a crown on our heads.*

R. *The Lord is kind and merciful.*

*How great is God's love for all
who worship him?
Greater than the distance
between heaven and earth!
How far has the L*ORD *taken
our sins from us?
Farther than the distance
from east to west!*

R. *The Lord is kind and merciful.*

SECOND READING

Romans 14:7–9

Whether alive or dead, we belong to the Lord.

A reading from the letter of Paul to the Romans

Brothers and sisters:
Whether we live or die,
it must be for God, rather than for ourselves.
Whether we live or die,
it must be for the Lord.
Alive or dead,
we still belong to the Lord.
This is because Christ died and rose to life,
so that he would be the Lord of the dead and of the living.

The word of the Lord.

Alleluia

John 13:34

R. *Alleluia, alleluia.*

*I give you a new commandment:
love one another as I have loved you.*

R. *Alleluia, alleluia.*

✠ A reading from the holy gospel according to Matthew

GOSPEL

Matthew 18:21–35

Peter came up to the Lord and asked,
"How many times should I forgive someone
   who does something wrong to me?
Is seven times enough?"

Jesus answered:
"Not just seven times, but seventy-seven times!
This story will show you
   what the kingdom of heaven is like:

I did not say to you to forgive seven times, but seventy times seven.

"One day a king decided to call in his officials
   and ask them to give an account of what they owed him.
As he was doing this,
one official was brought in
   who owed him fifty million silver coins.
But he didn't have any money to pay what he owed.
The king ordered him to be sold,
   along with his wife and children and all he owned,
   in order to pay the debt.

"The official got down on his knees and began begging,
'Have pity on me, and I will pay you every cent I owe!'
The king felt sorry for him and let him go free.
He even told the official
   that he did not have to pay back the money.

"As the official was leaving,
he happened to meet another official,
   who owed him a hundred silver coins.
So he grabbed the man by the throat.
He started choking him and said, 'Pay me what you owe!'

continued

"The man got down on his knees and began begging,
'Have pity on me, and I will pay you back.'
But the first official refused to have pity.
Instead, he went and had the other official put in jail
until he could pay what he owed.

"When some other officials found out what had happened,
they felt sorry for the man who had been put in jail.

"Then they told the king what had happened.
The king called the first official back in and said,
'You're an evil man!
When you begged for mercy,
I said you did not have to pay back a cent.
Don't you think you should show pity to someone else,
as I did to you?'

"The king was so angry
   that he ordered the official to be tortured
until he could pay back everything he owed.
That is how my Father in heaven will treat you,
if you don't forgive each of my followers
   with all your heart."

The gospel of the Lord.

TWENTY-FOURTH SUNDAY IN ORDINARY TIME

TWENTY-FIFTH SUNDAY IN ORDINARY TIME

FIRST READING | **A reading from the book of the prophet Isaiah**

Isaiah 55:6–9

My thoughts are not your thoughts.

Turn to the LORD!
He can still be found.
Call out to him.
He is near.
Give up your wicked ways and your evil thoughts.
Return to the LORD our God.
He will be merciful and forgive all your sins.

The LORD says: "My thoughts and my ways
   are not like yours.
Just as the heavens are higher than the earth,
my thoughts and my ways are higher than yours."

The word of the Lord.

Responsorial Psalm

R. *The Lord is near
to all who call on him.*

*LORD, I will praise you each day
and always honor your name.*

Psalm 145:2–3, 8–9, 17–18
(18a)

*You are wonderful, LORD,
and you deserve all praise,
because you are much greater
than anyone can understand.*

R. *The Lord is near
to all who call on him.*

*You are merciful, LORD!
You are kind and patient
and always loving.
You are good to everyone,
and you take care
of all your creation.*

R. *The Lord is near
to all who call on him.*

*Our LORD, everything you do
is kind and thoughtful,
and you are near to everyone
whose prayers are sincere.*

R. *The Lord is near
to all who call on him.*

Alleluia　　　　R. *Alleluia, alleluia.*

See Acts 16:14b　　*Open our hearts, O Lord,*
　　　　　　　　　to listen to the words of your Son.

　　　　　　　　　R. *Alleluia, alleluia.*

GOSPEL　　✢ **A reading from the holy gospel according to Matthew**

Matthew 20:1–16a

As Jesus was telling what the kingdom of heaven
　　would be like, he said:

"Early one morning a man went out
　　to hire some workers for his vineyard.
After he had agreed to pay them
　　the usual amount for a day's work,
he sent them off to his vineyard.

Are you jealous because I am generous!

"About nine that morning,
the man saw some other people
　　standing in the market with nothing to do.
He said he would pay them what was fair,
if they would work in his vineyard.
So they went.

"At noon and again about three in the afternoon
　　he returned to the market.
And each time he made the same agreement
　　with others who were loafing around with nothing to do.

"Finally, about five in the afternoon
　　the man went back and found some others standing there.
He asked them,
'Why have you been standing here all day long
　　doing nothing?'

"'Because no one has hired us,' they answered.
Then he told them to go work in his vineyard.

"That evening the owner of the vineyard
   told the man in charge of the workers
   to call them in and give them their money.
He also told the man to begin
   with the ones who were hired last.
When the workers arrived,
the ones who had been hired at five in the afternoon
   were given a full day's pay.

"The workers who had been hired first
   thought they would be given more than the others.
But when they were given the same,
they began complaining to the owner of the vineyard.
They said, 'The ones who were hired last
   worked for only one hour.
But you paid them the same that you did us.
And we worked in the hot sun all day long!'

"The owner answered one of them,
'Friend, I didn't cheat you.
I paid you exactly what we agreed on.
Take your money now and go!
What business is it of yours if I want to pay them
   the same that I paid you?
Don't I have the right to do what I want
   with my own money?
Why should you be jealous, if I want to be generous?'"

Jesus then said, "So it is!
Everyone who is now first will be last."

The gospel of the Lord.

TWENTY-SIXTH SUNDAY IN ORDINARY TIME

FIRST READING

A reading from the book of the prophet Ezekiel

Ezekiel 18:25–28

The sinner who decides to turn against sinfulness deserves to live.

The Lord says this:
People of Israel, you say,
"The Lord isn't fair!"
But you are the ones who are wrong.

I am fair,
and if any of you stop doing right and start sinning,
you will die because of your sins.
But if any of you turn from your sins and start doing right,
you will be safe.
You won't die because of your sins,
if you really think about the things you have done wrong
   and turn from them.

Do this, and you will go on living.

The word of the Lord.

Responsorial Psalm R. *Remember your mercies, O Lord.*

Psalm 25:4–5, 6–7, 8–9
(6a)

Show me your paths
and teach me to follow;
guide me by your truth
and instruct me.
You keep me safe,
and I always trust you.

R. *Remember your mercies, O Lord.*

Please, LORD, remember,
you have always
been patient and kind.
Forget each wrong I did
when I was young.
Show how truly kind you are
and remember me.

R. *Remember your mercies, O Lord.*

You are honest and merciful,
and you teach sinners
how to follow your path.
You lead humble people
to do what is right
and to stay on your path.

R. *Remember your mercies, O Lord.*

Second Reading

Philippians 2:1–5

In your minds be as Christ Jesus.

A reading from the letter of Paul to the Philippians

Brothers and sisters:
Christ encourages you,
and his love comforts you.
God's Spirit unites you,
and you are concerned for others.
Now make me completely happy!
Live in harmony by showing love for each other.
Be united in what you think,
as if you were only one person.

Don't be jealous or proud,
but be humble and consider others
    more important than yourselves.
Care about them as much as you care about yourselves
and think the same way that Christ Jesus did.

The word of the Lord.

Alleluia

John 10:27

R. Alleluia, alleluia.

*My sheep listen to my voice,
says the Lord;
I know them, and they follow me.*

R. Alleluia, alleluia.

Gospel

Matthew 21:28–32

✝ A reading from the holy gospel according to Matthew

Jesus said:
"I will tell you a story about a man who had two sons.
Then you can tell me what you think.

"The father went to the older son and said,
'Go work in the vineyard today!'
His son told him that he would not do it,
but later he changed his mind and went.
The man then told his younger son
   to go work in the vineyard.
The boy said he would, but he didn't go.
Which one of the sons obeyed his father?"

"The older one," the chief priests and leaders answered.

Then Jesus told them:
"You can be sure that tax collectors and bad women
   will get into the kingdom of God before you ever will!
When John the Baptist showed you how to do right,
you would not believe him.
But these evil people did believe.
And even when you saw what they did,
you still would not change your minds and believe."

The gospel of the Lord.

The son went out moved by regret.

TWENTY-SEVENTH SUNDAY IN ORDINARY TIME

FIRST READING

A reading from the book of the prophet Isaiah

Isaiah 5:1–7

I will sing a song about the vineyard of my dear friend.
It was on the side of a fertile hill.
My friend dug the ground, removed the stones,
  and planted the best vines.
He built a watchtower and dug a place to press the grapes.
He hoped they would be good,
but bitter grapes were all that grew.

The vineyard of the Lord God of hosts is the house of Israel.

Now listen, people of Jerusalem and of Judah!
You be the judge of me and my vineyard.
What more could I have done for my vineyard?
I hoped for good grapes,
but bitter grapes were all that grew.

Now I will tell you what I am going to do.
I will cut down the hedge and tear down the wall.
My vineyard will be trampled and left in ruins.
It will turn into a desert, neither tended nor hoed,
and it will be covered with thorns and briars.
I will command the clouds not to send it rain.

Israel is the vineyard of the LORD All-Powerful.
Judah is the garden that makes him rejoice.
He had hoped for honesty and for justice,
but dishonesty and crying were all he found.

The word of the Lord.

Responsorial Psalm

R. *The vineyard of the Lord
is the house of Israel.*

*Psalm 80:8 and 11,
14de–15ab and 19
(Isaiah 5:7a)*

*We were like a grapevine
you brought out of Egypt.
You chased other nations away
and planted us here.
Its branches stretched to the sea;
its new growth reached
to the river.*

R. *The vineyard of the Lord
is the house of Israel.*

*See what's happening
to this vine.
With your own hands
you planted its roots.
L*ORD* God All-Powerful,
make us strong again!
Smile on us and save us.*

R. *The vineyard of the Lord
is the house of Israel.*

A reading from the letter of Paul to the Philippians

SECOND READING

Philippians 4:6–9

Brothers and sisters:
Don't worry about anything,
but pray about everything.

With thankful hearts
   offer up your prayers and requests to God.
Then, because you belong to Christ Jesus,
God will bless you with peace
   that no one can completely understand.
And this peace will control the way you think and feel.

*Do these things,
and the God of peace
will be with you.*

continued

Finally, my friends,
keep your minds on whatever is true, pure, right,
   holy, friendly, and proper.
Don't ever stop thinking about what is truly worthwhile
   and worthy of praise.
You know the teachings I gave you,
and you know what you heard me say and saw me do.

So follow my example.
And God, who gives peace, will be with you.

The word of the Lord.

Alleluia   R. *Alleluia, alleluia.*

See John 15:16   *I have chosen you from the world,*
                        says the Lord,
                        to go and bear fruit that will last.

                        R. *Alleluia, alleluia.*

GOSPEL   ✠ **A reading from the holy gospel according to Matthew**

Matthew 21:33–43   Jesus told the chief priests and leaders to listen to this story:

A landowner leased his vineyard to other farmers.   "A land owner once planted a vineyard.
He built a wall around it and dug a pit to crush the grapes in.
He also built a lookout tower.

"Then he rented out his vineyard and left the country.

"When it was harvest time,
the owner sent some servants to get his share of the grapes.
But the renters grabbed those servants.
They beat up one, killed one,
   and stoned one of them to death.
He then sent more servants than he did the first time.
But the renters treated them in the same way.

"Finally, the owner sent his own son to the renters,
because he thought they would respect him.
But when they saw the man's son, they said,
'Someday he will own the vineyard.
Let's kill him!
Then we can have it all for ourselves.'
So they grabbed him, threw him out of the vineyard,
   and killed him."

Jesus asked, "When the owner of that vineyard comes,
what do you suppose he will do to those renters?"

The chief priests and leaders answered,
"He will kill them in some horrible way.
Then he will rent out his vineyard to people
   who will give him his share of grapes at harvest time."

Jesus replied, "Surely you know that the Scriptures say,

   'The stone that the builders tossed aside
   is now the most important stone of all.
   This is something the Lord has done,
   and it is amazing to us.'

"I tell you that God's kingdom will be taken from you
   and given to people who will do what he demands."

The gospel of the Lord.

TWENTY-EIGHTH SUNDAY IN ORDINARY TIME

FIRST READING | **A reading from the book of the prophet Isaiah**

Isaiah 25:6–10a

The Lord will prepare a feast and will wipe away the tears from every cheek.

On this mountain the LORD All-Powerful
   will prepare for all nations a feast of the finest foods.
Choice wines and the best meat will be served.
Here the LORD will strip away
   the funeral clothes that cover the nations.
The LORD All-Powerful will destroy the power of death
   and wipe away each tear.
No longer will his people be embarrassed everywhere.
The LORD has spoken!

On that day, people will say,
"The LORD God has saved us!
Let's celebrate.
We waited and waited, and now he is here."

The powerful arm of the LORD will protect this mountain.

The word of the Lord.

Responsorial Psalm

Psalm 23:1–3a,
4abcd and 5ac, 6
(6cd)

R. *I shall live in the house of the Lord*
all the days of my life.

You, LORD, are my shepherd.
I will never be in need.
You let me rest in fields
of green grass.
You lead me to streams
of peaceful water,
and you refresh my life.

R. *I shall live in the house of the Lord*
all the days of my life.

I may walk through valleys
as dark as death,
but I won't be afraid.
You are with me.
You treat me to a feast,
and you honor me as your guest.

R. *I shall live in the house of the Lord*
all the days of my life.

Your kindness and love
will always be with me
each day of my life,
and I will live forever
in your house, LORD.

R. *I shall live in the house of the Lord*
all the days of my life.

Second Reading

Philippians 4:12–14, 19–20

I am able to do all things in Christ who strengthens me.

A reading from the letter of Paul to the Philippians

Brothers and sisters:
I know what it is to be poor or to have plenty,
and I have lived under all kinds of conditions.
I know what it means to be full or to be hungry,
to have too much or too little.
Christ gives me the strength to face anything.

It was good of you to help me
    when I was having such a hard time.

I pray that God will take care of all your needs
    with the wonderful blessings that come from Christ Jesus!
May God our Father be praised forever and ever. Amen.

The word of the Lord.

Alleluia

See Ephesians 1:17–18

R. Alleluia, alleluia.

May the Father
of our Lord Jesus Christ
enlighten the eyes of our heart,
that we might see
how great is the hope
to which we are called.

R. Alleluia, alleluia.

GOSPEL

Matthew 22:1–10

✛ A reading from the holy gospel according to Matthew

Jesus used this story to teach the people:

"The kingdom of heaven is like what happened
when a king gave a wedding banquet for his son.
The king sent some servants to tell the invited guests
 to come to the banquet,
but the guests refused.
He sent other servants to say to the guests,
'The banquet is ready!
My cattle and prize calves have all been prepared.
Everything is ready.
Come to the banquet!'

"But the guests did not pay any attention.
Some of them left for their farms,
and some went to their places of business.
Others grabbed the servants, beat them up, and killed them.

"This made the king so furious that he sent an army to kill
 those murderers and burn down their city.
Then he said to the servants,
'It is time for the wedding banquet,
and the invited guests don't deserve to come.
Go out to the street corners and tell everyone you meet
 to come to the banquet.'
They went out on the streets
 and brought in everyone they could find,
 good and bad alike.
And the banquet room was filled with guests."

The gospel of the Lord.

Whomsoever you find invite to the wedding.

TWENTY-NINTH SUNDAY IN ORDINARY TIME

FIRST READING

A reading from the book of the prophet Isaiah

Isaiah 45:1, 4–6

I have taken the hand of Cyrus to subdue nations before his countenance.

The LORD said to Cyrus, his chosen one,
"I have taken hold of your right hand
  to help you conquer nations
  and remove kings from power.
City gates will open for you.
Not one will stay closed.

"Cyrus, you don't even know me!
But I have called you by name and highly honored you,
because of Jacob, my servant,
and Israel, my chosen one.
Only I am the LORD!

"There is no other God.
I have made you strong,
though you don't know me.
Now everyone from east to west
  will know that I am the LORD.
No other gods are real."

The word of the Lord.

Responsorial Psalm   R. *Give the Lord glory and honor.*

*Sing a new song to the L*ORD*!*
Everyone on this earth,
*sing praises to the L*ORD*.*
Tell every nation on earth,
*"The L*ORD *is wonderful*
and does marvelous things!"

Psalm 96:1 and 3, 4–5, 9–10abef
(7b)

R. *Give the Lord glory and honor.*

*"The L*ORD *is great and deserves*
our greatest praise!
He is the only God
worthy of our worship.
Other nations worship idols,
*but the L*ORD *created the heavens."*

R. *Give the Lord glory and honor.*

"Everyone on earth, now tremble
*and worship the L*ORD*,*
majestic and holy."
Announce to the nations,
*"The L*ORD *is King!*
God will judge the people
with fairness."

R. *Give the Lord glory and honor.*

Second Reading

1 Thessalonians 1:1–5b

We are mindful of your faith, hope, and love.

A reading from the first letter of Paul to the Thessalonians

From Paul, Silas, and Timothy.
To the church in Thessalonica,
    the people of God the Father and of the Lord Jesus Christ.

I pray that God will be kind to you
    and will bless you with peace!

We thank God for you
    and always mention you in our prayers.
Each time we pray,
we tell God our Father about your faith and loving work
    and about your firm hope in our Lord Jesus Christ.

My dear friends, God loves you,
and we know he has chosen you to be his people.
When we told you the good news,
it was with the power and assurance
    that come from the Holy Spirit,
    and not simply with words.

The word of the Lord.

Alleluia

Philippians 2:15d, 16a

R. *Alleluia, alleluia.*

Shine on the world like bright stars;
you are offering it the word of life.

R. *Alleluia, alleluia.*

Gospel

Matthew 22:15–21

✢ **A reading from the holy gospel according to Matthew**

The Pharisees got together
   and planned how they could trick Jesus
   into saying something wrong.
They sent some of their followers
   and some of Herod's followers to say to him,
"Teacher, we know that you are honest.
You teach the truth about what God wants people to do.
And you treat everyone with the same respect,
no matter who they are.
Tell us what you think!
Should we pay taxes to the Emperor or not?"

Jesus knew their evil thoughts and said,
"Why are you trying to test me? You showoffs!
Let me see one of the coins used for paying taxes."

They brought him a silver coin, and he asked,
"Whose picture and name are on it?"

"The Emperor's," they answered.

Then Jesus told them,
"Give the Emperor what belongs to him
and give God what belongs to God."

The gospel of the Lord.

Give to Caesar the things that belong to Caesar and to God the things that are God's.

THIRTIETH SUNDAY IN ORDINARY TIME

FIRST READING

A reading from the first letter of Paul to the Thessalonians

1 Thessalonians 1:5–8a

You turned away from idols to serve God and await his Son.

Brothers and sisters:
When we told you the good news,
it was with the power and assurance
    that come from the Holy Spirit,
    and not simply with words.

You knew what kind of people we were
    and how we helped you.
So, when you accepted the message,
you followed our example and the example of the Lord.
You suffered, but the Holy Spirit made you glad.

You became an example for all the Lord's followers
    in Macedonia and Achaia.
And because of you,
the Lord's message has spread everywhere in those regions.

The word of the Lord.

Responsorial Psalm R. *I love you, Lord, my strength.*

*I love you, LORD God,
and you make me strong.
You are my mighty rock,
my fortress, my protector,
the rock where I am safe,
my shield, my powerful weapon,
and my place of shelter.*

Psalm 18:1–2, 46 and 50ce
(2)

R. *I love you, Lord, my strength.*

*You are the living LORD!
I will praise you.
You are a mighty rock.
I will honor you
for keeping me safe.
Your faithful love for David
will never end.*

R. *I love you, Lord, my strength.*

Alleluia R. *Alleluia, alleluia.*

John 14:23

All who love me will keep my words,
and my Father will love them,
and we will come to them.

R. *Alleluia, alleluia.*

GOSPEL

✠ **A reading from the holy gospel according to Matthew**

Matthew 22:34–40

After Jesus had made the Sadducees look foolish,
the Pharisees heard about it and got together.
One of them was an expert in the Jewish Law.
So he tried to test Jesus by asking,
"Teacher, what is the most important commandment
   in the Law?"

Love the Lord your God, and your neighbor as yourself.

Jesus answered:
"'Love the Lord your God with all your heart, soul,
   and mind.'
This is the first and most important commandment.
The second most important commandment is like this one.
And it is, 'Love others as much as you love yourself.'
All the Law of Moses and the Books of the Prophets
   are based on these two commandments."

The gospel of the Lord.

THIRTIETH SUNDAY IN ORDINARY TIME

THIRTY-FIRST SUNDAY IN ORDINARY TIME

FIRST READING

Malachi 2:8–10

You have strayed from the way, you have caused many to stumble by your teaching.

A reading from the book of the prophet Malachi

The LORD says this:
Although I am the LORD All-Powerful,
you priests have turned from following me.
Your teachings have led many people to do sinful things,
and you have broken the promise that Levi made to me.

So I made everyone hate and despise you
because you disobeyed me and did not treat all people alike.

Don't you know that we all have the same father?
Didn't the one God create us all?
So why do you cheat each other
   by breaking the promise that your ancestors made?

The word of the Lord.

Responsorial Psalm R. Teach me your ways, O Lord.

*Show me your paths
and teach me to follow;
guide me by your truth
and instruct me.
You keep me safe.*

*Psalm 25:4–5abc,
6 and 7cd, 8–9 (4a)*

R. Teach me your ways, O Lord.

*Please, LORD, remember,
you have always
been patient and kind.
Show how truly kind you are
and remember me.*

R. Teach me your ways, O Lord.

*You are honest and merciful,
and you teach sinners
how to follow your path.
You lead humble people
to do what is right
and to stay on your path.*

R. Teach me your ways, O Lord.

Second Reading

1 Thessalonians 2:7–9, 13

A reading from the first letter of Paul to the Thessalonians

Brothers and sisters:
We could have demanded help from you.
After all, Christ is the one who sent us.
We chose to be like children
    or like a mother nursing her baby.
We cared so much for you,
and you became so dear to us,
that we were willing to give our lives for you
    when we gave you God's message.

My dear friends,
you surely haven't forgotten our hard work and hardships.
You remember how night and day
    we struggled to make a living,
so that we could tell you God's message
    without being a burden to anyone.

We always thank God
    that you believed the message we preached.
It came from him,
and it is not something made up by humans.
You accepted it as God's message,
and now he is working in you.

The word of the Lord.

We were eager to hand over to you not only the good news but our lives as well.

Alleluia

Matthew 23:9b, 10b

R. *Alleluia, alleluia.*

*You have one Father,
your Father in heaven;
you have one teacher,
the Lord Jesus Christ!*

R. *Alleluia, alleluia.*

GOSPEL

Matthew 23:1–12

✠ A reading from the holy gospel according to Matthew

Jesus said to the crowds and to his disciples:
"The Pharisees and the teachers of the Law
 are experts in the Law of Moses.
So obey everything they teach you,
but don't do as they do.
After all, they say one thing and do something else.

"They pile heavy burdens on people's shoulders
 and won't lift a finger to help them.
Everything they do is just to show off in front of others.
They even make a big show
 of wearing Scripture verses on their foreheads and arms,
and they wear big tassels for everyone to see.
They love the best seats at banquets
 and the front seats in the meeting places.
And when they are in the market,
they like to have people greet them as their teachers.

"But none of you should be called a teacher.
You have only one teacher,
and all of you are like brothers and sisters.
Don't call anyone on earth your father.
All of you have the same Father in heaven.
None of you should be called the leader.
The Messiah is your only leader.

"Whoever is the greatest should be the servant of the others.
If you put yourself above others,
you will be put down.
But if you humble yourself,
you will be honored."

The gospel of the Lord.

The scribes and the Pharisees do not practice what they preach.

THIRTY-SECOND SUNDAY IN ORDINARY TIME

First Reading

Wisdom 6:12–16

Wisdom is found by those who look for it.

A reading from the book of Wisdom

Wisdom shines brightly,
and she is easily seen by all who love her
　　and search for her.

Wisdom hurries to meet everyone who wants to be wise.
If you get up early and search,
you will easily find her at your front door.

Keep your mind on Wisdom,
and you will be very wise.
Keep thinking about her,
and all of your worries will soon disappear.

Wisdom goes around searching for those who deserve her.
She meets them along the road and stays in their thoughts.

The word of the Lord.

Responsorial Psalm

R. *My soul is thirsting for you,*
O Lord my God.

Psalm 63:1, 2–3, 6–7
(2b)

You are my God. I worship you.
In my heart, I long for you,
as I would long for a stream
in a scorching desert.

R. *My soul is thirsting for you,*
O Lord my God.

I have seen your power
and your glory
in the place of worship.
Your love means more
than life to me,
and so I praise you.

R. *My soul is thirsting for you,*
O Lord my God.

I think about you
before I go to sleep,
and my thoughts turn to you
during the night.
You have helped me,
and I sing happy songs
in the shadow of your wings.

R. *My soul is thirsting for you,*
O Lord my God.

Second Reading

1 Thessalonians 4:13–18

Those who died, God will bring to life with Jesus.

A reading from the first letter of Paul to the Thessalonians

Brothers and sisters:
My friends, we want you to understand how it will be
    for those followers who have already died.
Then you won't grieve over them
    and be like people who don't have any hope.

We believe that Jesus died and was raised to life.
We also believe that when God brings Jesus back again,
he will bring with him
    all who had faith in Jesus before they died.
Our Lord Jesus told us that when he comes,
we won't go up to meet him
    ahead of his followers who have already died.

With a loud command and with the shout of the chief angel
    and a blast of God's trumpet,
the Lord will return from heaven.
Then those who had faith in Christ before they died
    will be raised to life.
Next, all of us who are still alive
    will be taken up into the clouds together with them
    to meet the Lord in the sky.
From that time on we will all be with the Lord forever.

Encourage each other with these words.

The word of the Lord.

Alleluia

Matthew 24:42a, 44

R. *Alleluia, alleluia.*

*Be watchful and ready:
you know not when
the Son of Man is coming.*

R. *Alleluia, alleluia.*

✢ A reading from the holy gospel according to Matthew

GOSPEL

Jesus told his disciples this story
   about the kingdom of heaven:

Matthew 25:1–13

"The kingdom of heaven is like what happened one night
   when ten girls took their oil lamps
   and went to a wedding to meet the groom.
Five of the girls were foolish and five were wise.
The foolish ones took their lamps, but no extra oil.
The ones who were wise took along extra oil for their lamps.

Look, the bridegroom comes.
Go out to meet him.

"The groom was late arriving,
and the girls became drowsy and fell asleep.
Then in the middle of the night someone shouted,
'Here's the groom! Come to meet him!'

"When the girls got up and started getting their lamps ready,
the foolish ones said to the others,
'Let us have some of your oil!
Our lamps are going out.'

"The girls who were wise answered,
'There's not enough oil for all of us!
Go and buy some for yourselves.'

"While the foolish girls were on their way to get some oil,
the groom arrived.
The girls who were ready went into the wedding,
and the doors were closed.
Later the other girls returned and shouted,
'Sir, sir! Open the door for us!'

"But the groom replied, 'I don't even know you!'

"So, my disciples, always be ready!
You don't know the day or the time
when all this will happen."

The gospel of the Lord.

THIRTY-THIRD SUNDAY IN ORDINARY TIME

FIRST READING

A reading from the first letter of Paul to the Thessalonians

1 Thessalonians 5:1–6

The day of the Lord is going to come like a thief in the night.

Brothers and sisters:
I don't need to write you
 about the time or date when all this will happen.
You surely know that the Lord's return
 will be as a thief coming at night.
People will think they are safe and secure.
But destruction will suddenly strike them
 like the pains of a woman about to give birth.
And they won't escape.

My dear friends, you don't live in darkness,
and so that day won't surprise you like a thief.
All of you belong to the light and live in the day.
We don't live in the night or belong to the dark.
Others may sleep,
but we should stay awake and be alert.

The word of the Lord.

Responsorial Psalm   R. The Lord is my light and my salvation.

Psalm 27:1, 13–14
(1a)

*You, LORD, are the light
that keeps me safe.
I am not afraid of anyone.
You protect me,
and I have no fears.*

R. The Lord is my light and my salvation.

*LORD, I know I will live
to see how kind you are.
Trust the LORD!
Be brave and strong
and trust the LORD.*

R. The Lord is my light and my salvation.

Alleluia   R. Alleluia, alleluia.

John 15:4a, 5b

*Live in me and let me live in you,
says the Lord;
my branches bear much fruit.*

R. Alleluia, alleluia.

GOSPEL

Matthew 25:14–15, 19–21

Because you have been faithful in small matters, come into the joy of your master.

✠ **A reading from the holy gospel according to Matthew**

Jesus told his disciples this story about the kingdom of God:

"The kingdom is like what happened
   when a man went away
   and put his three servants in charge of all he owned.
The man knew what each servant could do.
So he handed five thousand coins to the first servant,
two thousand to the second,
and one thousand to the third.
Then he left the country.

"Some time later the master of those servants returned.
He called them in
   and asked what they had done with his money.
The servant who had been given five thousand coins
   brought them in with the five thousand
   that he had earned.
He said, 'Sir, you gave me five thousand coins,
and I have earned five thousand more.'

"'Wonderful!' his master replied,
'You are a good and faithful servant.
I left you in charge of only a little,
but now I will put you in charge of much more.
Come and share in my happiness!'"

The gospel of the Lord.

CHRIST THE KING
Thirty-Fourth or Last Sunday in Ordinary Time

First Reading

Ezekiel 34:11–12, 14–16abce

The Lord will shepherd his flock.

A reading from the book of the prophet Ezekiel

The Lord says this:
"I, the Lord God, will look for my people
 and take care of them myself.
As a shepherd looks for sheep that have wandered away,
I will search for my scattered people.
I will rescue them from all the places where they went
 on that dark and gloomy day.

"My people will be like sheep grazing and resting
 in good pastures and on Israel's mountains.
I, the Lord All-Powerful,
 will lead them there and watch over them.

"I will look for the lost sheep
 and bring back the ones that have wandered off.
If any are hurt,
I will bandage their wounds.
If any are weak,
I will help them.
I will take good care of my people!"

The word of the Lord.

Responsorial Psalm

R. *The Lord is my shepherd;*
there is nothing I shall want.

Psalm 23:1–2ab, 2c–3, 5–6
(1)

You, LORD, are my shepherd.
I will never be in need.
You let me rest in fields
of green grass.

R. *The Lord is my shepherd;*
there is nothing I shall want.

You lead me to streams
of peaceful water,
and you refresh my life.
You are true to your name,
and you lead me
along the right paths.

R. *The Lord is my shepherd;*
there is nothing I shall want.

You treat me to a feast,
while my enemies watch.
You honor me as your guest,
and you fill my cup
until it overflows.
Your kindness and love
will always be with me
each day of my life,
and I will live forever
in your house, LORD.

R. *The Lord is my shepherd;*
there is nothing I shall want.

Second Reading

1 Corinthians 15:20–24a

Christ will hand over the kingdom to God the Father.

A reading from the first letter of Paul to the Corinthians

Brothers and sisters:
Christ has been raised to life!
And he makes us certain
that others will also be raised to life.

Just as we will die because of Adam,
we will be raised to life because of Christ.
Adam brought death to all of us,
and Christ will bring life to all of us.

But we must each wait our turn.
Christ was the first to be raised to life,
and his people will be raised to life when he returns.
Then after Christ has destroyed all powers and forces,
the end will come.

The word of the Lord.

Alleluia

Mark 11:9, 10

R. Alleluia, alleluia.

*Blessed is the one who inherits
the kingdom of David our father;
blessed is the one who comes
in the name of the Lord.*

R. Alleluia, alleluia.

GOSPEL

Matthew 25:31–46

✚ **A reading from the holy gospel according to Matthew**

Jesus said to his disciples:
"When the Son of Man comes in his glory
 with all of his angels,
he will sit on his royal throne.

"The people of all nations will be brought before him,
and he will separate them,
as shepherds separate their sheep from their goats.

The Son of Man will sit upon his seat of glory and he will separate all into two groups.

"He will place the sheep on his right
 and the goats on his left.
Then the king will say to those on his right,
'My father has blessed you!
Come and receive the kingdom that was prepared for you
 before the world was created.
When I was hungry, you gave me something to eat,
and when I was thirsty, you gave me something to drink.
When I was a stranger, you welcomed me,
and when I was naked, you gave me clothes to wear.
When I was sick, you took care of me,
and when I was in jail, you visited me.'

"Then the ones who pleased the Lord will ask,
'When did we give you something to eat or drink?
When did we welcome you as a stranger
 or give you clothes to wear
 or visit you while you were sick or in jail?'

"The king will answer,
'Whenever you did it for any of my people,
 no matter how unimportant they seemed,
you did it for me.'

continued

"Then the king will say to those on his left,
'Get away from me!
You are under God's curse.
Go into the everlasting fire
   prepared for the devil and his angels!
I was hungry, but you did not give me anything to eat,
and I was thirsty, but you did not give me anything to drink.
I was a stranger, but you did not welcome me,
and I was naked,
   but you did not give me any clothes to wear.
I was sick and in jail, but you did not take care of me.'

"Then the people will ask,
'Lord, when did we fail to help you
   when you were hungry or thirsty
   or a stranger or naked or sick or in jail?'

"The king will say to them,
'Whenever you failed to help any of my people,
   no matter how unimportant they seemed,
you failed to do it for me.'"

Then Jesus said, "Those people will be punished forever.
But the ones who pleased God will have eternal life."

The gospel of the Lord.

CHRIST THE KING

Solemnities of the Lord during Ordinary Time

HOLY TRINITY
Sunday after Pentecost

First Reading

A reading from the book of Exodus

Exodus 34:4b–6, 8–9

The Lord God, ruler of all, merciful and loving.

Moses did exactly what the Lord had told him.
He got up early and carried the two stone tablets
  up the side of Mount Sinai.

The Lord came down in a cloud and stood beside Moses.
Then he said, "I am the Lord."
He also walked up and down in front of Moses and said,
"I am the Lord God,
and I am kind and merciful.
I don't easily lose my temper,
and my love can be trusted."

Moses quickly bowed low.
He worshiped and said,
"Lord, if you are pleased with me,
then don't leave your people.
We are stubborn.
But I beg you to forgive our terrible sins
and let us be your very own people."

The word of the Lord.

Responsorial Psalm   R. Glory and praise for ever!

*Lord God of our ancestors,
you are worthy of praise,
the highest praise forever.*

Daniel 3:52, 53 and 56 (52b)

*Your glorious and holy name
is also worthy of praise,
the highest praise forever.*

R. *Glory and praise for ever!*

*You are glorious and holy,
worthy of praise in your temple,
the highest praise forever.
You are worthy of praise
in the heavens,
honored with hymns forever.*

R. *Glory and praise for ever!*

Second Reading

2 Corinthians 13:11–13

The grace of our Lord Jesus Christ and the love of God and the fellowship of the Holy Spirit be with you all.

A reading from the second letter of Paul to the Corinthians

Good-bye, my friends.
Do better and pay attention to what I have said.
Try to get along and live peacefully with each other.

Now I pray that God,
    who gives love and peace,
    will be with you.
Give each other a warm greeting.
All of God's people send their greetings.

I pray that the Lord Jesus Christ
    will bless you and be kind to you!
May God bless you with his love,
and may the Holy Spirit join all your hearts together.

The word of the Lord.

Alleluia

See Revelation 1:8

R. *Alleluia, alleluia.*

*Glory to the Father, the Son,
and the Holy Spirit:
to God who is, who was,
and who is to come.*

R. *Alleluia, alleluia.*

✢ A reading from the holy gospel according to John

Jesus told Nicodemus:
"God loved the people of this world so much
 that he gave his only Son,
so that everyone who has faith in him
 will have eternal life and never die.
God did not send his Son into the world
 to condemn its people.
He sent him to save them!"

The gospel of the Lord.

GOSPEL

John 3:16–17

God sent his Son to save the world through him.

THE BODY AND BLOOD OF CHRIST
Sunday after Trinity Sunday

First Reading

A reading from the book of Deuteronomy

Deuteronomy 8:2–3, 14b–16a

The Lord gave you food that you and your ancestors did not know.

Moses told the people:
"Don't forget how the LORD your God
　led you in the desert for forty years.
The LORD did this
so that you would learn to depend on him.
And he wanted to know
if you were truly willing to obey him.

"The LORD made you go hungry.
Then he gave you manna,
a kind of food that you and your ancestors
　had never heard about.
He did this to teach you that people
　need more than food to live.
They need every word that the LORD has spoken.

"The LORD your God brought you out of Egypt,
where you were slaves.
He led you safely through a big and terrible desert
　that was full of poisonous snakes and scorpions.

"The LORD gave you water from solid rock.
And in the desert he gave you manna,
a kind of food your ancestors had never heard about.
He tested you like this to teach you to depend on him,
so that all would go well for you."

The word of the Lord.

Responsorial Psalm

R. *Praise the Lord, Jerusalem.*
or:
R. *Alleluia.*

Psalm 147:12 and 14, 19–20
(12)

Everyone in Jerusalem,
come and praise
the LORD *your God!*
God lets you live in peace,
and he gives you
the very best wheat.

R. *Praise the Lord, Jerusalem.*
or:
R. *Alleluia.*

God gave his laws and teachings
to the descendants of Jacob,
the nation of Israel.
But he has not given his laws
to any other nation.
Shout praises to the LORD*!*

R. *Praise the Lord, Jerusalem.*
or:
R. *Alleluia.*

SECOND READING

1 Corinthians 10:16–17

Though we are many, we are one bread.

A reading from the first letter of Paul to the Corinthians

Brothers and sisters:
When we drink from the cup that we ask God to bless,
isn't that sharing in the blood of Christ?
When we eat the bread that we break,
isn't that sharing in the body of Christ?
By sharing in the same loaf of bread,
we become one body,
even though there are many of us.

The word of the Lord.

Alleluia

John 6:51

R. Alleluia, alleluia.

*I am the living bread from heaven,
says the Lord;
whoever eats this bread
will live for ever.*

R. Alleluia, alleluia.

✠ A reading from the holy gospel according to John

Jesus said to the crowd:
"I am the bread from heaven!
Everyone who eats it will live forever.
My flesh is the life-giving bread
   that I give to the people of this world."

They started arguing with each other and asked,
"How can he give us his flesh to eat?"

Jesus answered:
"I tell you for certain that you won't live
unless you eat the flesh and drink the blood
   of the Son of Man.
But if you do eat my flesh and drink my blood,
you will have eternal life,
and I will raise you to life on the last day.

"My flesh is the true food,
and my blood is the true drink.
If you eat my flesh and drink my blood,
you are one with me, and I am one with you.

"The living Father sent me,
and I have life because of him.
Now everyone who eats my flesh will live because of me.

"The bread that comes down from heaven
   is not like what your ancestors ate.
They died,
but whoever eats this bread will live forever."

The gospel of the Lord.

GOSPEL

John 6:51–58

*My flesh is real food
and my blood is real drink.*

THE SACRED HEART OF JESUS
Friday after the Second Sunday after Pentecost

FIRST READING

A reading from the book of Deuteronomy

Deuteronomy 7:6–11

Moses told the people:
"You are the special people of the LORD your God.
The LORD has chosen you from all the people on earth
   to be his very own.
He wanted you and chose you,
even though you are not a powerful nation.
In fact, you are weaker than any other nation.

The Lord loves you and has chosen you.

"But the LORD had made a promise to your ancestors,
and he kept it by caring for you.
With his own mighty arm
he rescued you from the power of the king of Egypt,
who had made you his slaves.

"Don't forget that the LORD your God is the only God.
He can be trusted
   to keep his merciful promise for thousands of years
   to everyone who loves and obeys him.
But he quickly and completely destroys
   anyone who hates him.
So be sure to obey the laws, commands, and rules
   that I am teaching you today."

The word of the Lord.

Responsorial Psalm R. *The Lord's kindness is everlasting*
to those who fear him.

With all my heart
I praise the LORD,
Psalm 103:1–2, 3 and 5 *and with all that I am*
(see 17) *I praise his holy name!*
With all my heart
I praise the LORD!
I will never forget
how kind he has been.

R. *The Lord's kindness is everlasting*
to those who fear him.

The LORD forgives our sins
and heals us when we are sick.
Each day that we live,
he provides for our needs
and gives us the strength
of a young eagle.

R. *The Lord's kindness is everlasting*
to those who fear him.

SECOND READING

1 John 4:7–11, 16b

God loved us first.

A reading from the first letter of John

My dear friends, we must love each other.
Love comes from God,
and when we love each other,
it shows that we have been given new life.

We are now God's children, and we know him.

God is love,
and anyone who doesn't love others has never known him.

God showed his love for us
when he sent his only Son into the world to give us life.

Real love is not our love for God, but his love for us.
God sent his Son to be the sacrifice
  by which our sins are forgiven.

Dear friends,
since God loved us this much,
we must love each other.

God is love.
If we keep on loving others,
we will stay one in our hearts with God,
and he will stay one with us.

The word of the Lord.

Alleluia

Matthew 11:29ab

R. *Alleluia, alleluia.*

*Take my yoke upon you;
learn from me, for I am gentle
and humble of heart.*

R. *Alleluia, alleluia.*

GOSPEL

Matthew 11:25–30

✢ A reading from the holy gospel according to Matthew

On one occasion Jesus said:
"My Father, Lord of heaven and earth,
I am grateful that you hid all this
 from wise and educated people
 and showed it to ordinary people.
Yes, Father, that is what pleased you.

"My Father has given me everything,
and he is the only one who knows the Son.
The only one who truly knows the Father is the Son.
But the Son wants to tell others about the Father,
so that they can know him too.

"If you are tired from carrying heavy burdens,
come to me and I will give you rest.
Take the yoke I give you.
Put it on your shoulders and learn from me.
I am gentle and humble,
and you will find rest.
This yoke is easy to bear,
and this burden is light."

The gospel of the Lord.

*I am gentle
and humble of heart.*

Common Texts for Sung Responsorial Psalms

The psalm, as a rule, is drawn from the Lectionary because the individual psalm texts are directly connected with the individual readings: the choice of psalm depends therefore on the readings.

Nevertheless, in order that the children may be able to join in the responsorial psalm more readily, some texts of responses and psalms have been chosen, according to the different seasons of the year, for optional use, whenever the psalm is sung, in place of the text corresponding to the reading (see General Instruction of the Roman Missal, no. 36).

SEASON OF ADVENT

ONE

Psalm 25:4 – 5abc,
8 – 9, 10 and 14 *(1)*

R. *To you, O Lord, I lift my soul.*
or:
R. *Come, O Lord, and set us free.*

Show me your paths
and teach me to follow;
guide me by your truth
and instruct me.
You keep me safe.

R. *To you, O Lord, I lift my soul.*
or:
R. *Come, O Lord, and set us free.*

You are honest and merciful,
and you teach sinners
how to follow your path.
You lead humble people
to do what is right
and to stay on your path.

R. *To you, O Lord, I lift my soul.*
or:
R. *Come, O Lord, and set us free.*

In everything you do,
you are kind and faithful
to everyone who keeps
our agreement with you.
Our LORD, *you are the friend*
of your worshipers,
and you make an agreement
with all of us.

R. *To you, O Lord, I lift my soul.*
or:
R. *Come, O Lord, and set us free.*

TWO

Psalm 85:8 – 9,
10 – 11, 12 – 13 *(8a)*

R. *Lord, show us your mercy and love.*
or:
R. *Come, O Lord, and set us free.*

I will listen to you, LORD God,
because you promise peace
to those who are faithful
and no longer foolish.
You are ready to rescue
everyone who worships you,
so that you will live with us
in all of your glory.

R. *Lord, show us your mercy and love.*
or:
R. *Come, O Lord, and set us free.*

Love and loyalty
will come together;
goodness and peace will unite.
Loyalty will sprout
from the ground;
justice will look down
from the sky above.

R. *Lord, show us your mercy and love.*
or:
R. *Come, O Lord, and set us free.*

Our Lord, you will bless us;
our land will produce
wonderful crops.
Justice will march in front,
making a path
for you to follow.

R. *Lord, show us your mercy and love.*
or:
R. *Come, O Lord, and set us free.*

SEASON OF CHRISTMAS

ONE

Psalm 98:1, 2 – 3ab,
3cd – 4, 5–6 (3cd)

R. All the ends of the earth
have seen the saving power of God.
or:
R. Lord, today we have seen your glory.

Sing a new song to the LORD!
He has worked miracles,
and with his own powerful arm,
he has won the victory.

R. All the ends of the earth
have seen the saving power of God.
or:
R. Lord, today we have seen your glory.

The LORD has shown the nations
that he has the power to save
and to bring justice.
God has been faithful
in his love for Israel.

R. All the ends of the earth
have seen the saving power of God.
or:
R. Lord, today we have seen your glory.

His saving power is seen
everywhere on earth.
Tell everyone on this earth
to sing happy songs
in praise of the LORD.

R. All the ends of the earth
have seen the saving power of God.
or:
R. Lord, today we have seen your glory.

Make music for him on harps.
Play beautiful melodies!
Sound the trumpets and horns
and celebrate with joyful songs
for our LORD and King!

R. All the ends of the earth
have seen the saving power of God.
or:
R. Lord, today we have seen your glory.

SEASON OF LENT

ONE

**Psalm 51:1–2,
10–11, 12 and 15
(see 3a)**

R. Be merciful, O Lord, for we have sinned.
or:
R. Remember, O Lord, your faithfulness
and love.

*You are kind, God!
Please have pity on me.
You are always merciful!
Please wipe away my sins.
Wash me clean from all
of my sin and guilt.*

R. Be merciful, O Lord, for we have sinned.
or:
R. Remember, O Lord, your faithfulness
and love.

*Create pure thoughts in me
and make me faithful again.
Don't chase me away from you
or take your Holy Spirit
away from me.*

R. Be merciful, O Lord, for we have sinned.
or:
R. Remember, O Lord, your faithfulness
and love.

*Make me as happy as you did
when you saved me;
make me want to obey!
Help me to speak,
and I will praise you, Lord.*

R. Be merciful, O Lord, for we have sinned.
or:
R. Remember, O Lord, your faithfulness
and love.

TWO

**Psalm 91:1–2,
10–11, 14–15
(see 15b)**

R. Be with me, Lord, when I am in trouble.
or:
R. Remember, O Lord, your faithfulness
and love.

*Live under the protection
of God Most High
and stay in the shadow
of God All-Powerful.
Then you will say to the* L<small>ORD</small>,
*"You are my fortress,
my place of safety;
you are my God,
and I trust you."*

R. Be with me, Lord, when I am in trouble.
or:
R. Remember, O Lord, your faithfulness
and love.

*No terrible disasters
will strike you or your home.
God will command his angels
to protect you
wherever you go.*

R. Be with me, Lord, when I am in trouble.
or:
R. Remember, O Lord, your faithfulness
and love.

*The Lord says, "If you love me
and truly know who I am,
I will rescue you
and keep you safe.
When you are in trouble,
call out to me.
I will answer and be there
to protect and honor you."*

R. Be with me, Lord, when I am in trouble.
or:
R. Remember, O Lord, your faithfulness
and love.

THREE

**Psalm 130:1 – 2,
5 – 6ab, 6def, 7
(7bc)**

R. With the Lord there is mercy,
and fullness of redemption.
or:
R. Remember, O Lord, your faithfulness
and love.

From a sea of troubles
I call out to you, LORD.
Won't you please listen
as I beg for mercy?

R. With the Lord there is mercy,
and fullness of redemption.
or:
R. Remember, O Lord, your faithfulness
and love.

With all my heart,
I am waiting, LORD, for you!
I trust your promises.
I wait for you more eagerly
than a soldier on guard duty.

R. With the Lord there is mercy,
and fullness of redemption.
or:
R. Remember, O Lord, your faithfulness
and love.

Yes, I wait more eagerly
than a soldier on guard duty
waits for the dawn.

R. With the Lord there is mercy,
and fullness of redemption.
or:
R. Remember, O Lord, your faithfulness
and love.

Israel, trust the LORD!
He is always merciful,
and he has the power
to save you.

R. With the Lord there is mercy,
and fullness of redemption.
or:
R. Remember, O Lord, your faithfulness
and love.

SEASON OF EASTER

ONE

**Psalm 118:1–2,
15c–16ab, 17,
22–23 *(24)***

R. This is the day the Lord has made;
let us rejoice and be glad.
or:
R. Alleluia.

Tell the Lord
how thankful you are,
because he is kind
and always merciful.
Let Israel shout,
"God is always merciful!"

R. This is the day the Lord has made;
let us rejoice and be glad.
or:
R. Alleluia.

The Lord is powerful!
With his mighty arm
the Lord wins victories!

R. This is the day the Lord has made;
let us rejoice and be glad.
or:
R. Alleluia.

And so my life is safe,
and I will live to tell
what the Lord has done.

R. This is the day the Lord has made;
let us rejoice and be glad.
or:
R. Alleluia.

The stone that the builders
tossed aside
has now become
the most important stone.
The Lord has done this,
and it is amazing to us.

R. This is the day the Lord has made;
let us rejoice and be glad.
or:
R. Alleluia.

TWO

**Psalm 66:1 – 3a,
4 – 5, 6 – 7a** *(1)*

*R. Let all the earth cry out to God with joy,
alleluia.
or:
R. Alleluia.*

*Tell everyone on this earth
to shout praises to God!
Sing about his glorious name.
Honor him with praises.
Say to God, "Everything you do is fearsome!"*

*R. Let all the earth cry out to God with joy,
alleluia.
or:
R. Alleluia.*

*"You are worshiped by everyone!
We all sing praises to you."
Come and see the fearsome things
our God has done!*

*R. Let all the earth cry out to God with joy,
alleluia.
or:
R. Alleluia.*

*When God made the sea dry up,
our people walked across,
and because of him,
we celebrated there.
His mighty power rules forever.*

*R. Let all the earth cry out to God with joy,
alleluia.
or:
R. Alleluia.*

ORDINARY TIME

ONE

Psalm 19:7, 8
(John 6:68c)

R. Lord, you have the words of everlasting life.

The Law of the Lord is perfect;
it gives us new life.
His teachings last forever,
and they give wisdom to ordinary people.

R. Lord, you have the words of everlasting life.

The Lord's instruction is right;
it makes our hearts glad.
His commands shine brightly,
and they give us light.

R. Lord, you have the words of everlasting life.

TWO

Psalm 27:1, 4,
13–14 *(1a)*

R. The Lord is my light and my salvation.

You, Lord, are the light
that keeps me safe.
I am not afraid of anyone.
You protect me,
and I have no fears.

R. The Lord is my light and my salvation.

I ask only one thing, Lord:
Let me live in your house
every day of my life
to see how wonderful you are
and to pray in your temple.

R. The Lord is my light and my salvation.

I know that I will live
to see how kind you are.
Trust the Lord!
Be brave and strong
and trust the Lord.

R. The Lord is my light and my salvation.

THREE

**Psalm 34:1 – 2,
3 and 5, 7 – 8** *(2)*

R. *I will bless the Lord at all times.*

I will always praise the LORD.
*With all my heart,
I will praise the* LORD.
*Let all who are helpless
listen and be glad.*

R. *I will bless the Lord at all times.*

Honor the LORD *with me!
Celebrate his great name.
Keep your eyes on the* LORD*!
You will shine like the sun
and never blush with shame.*

R. *I will bless the Lord at all times.*

If you honor the LORD,
*his angel will protect you.
Discover for yourself
that the* LORD *is kind.
Come to him for protection,
and you will be glad.*

R. *I will bless the Lord at all times.*

FOUR

**Psalm 63:1, 2–3,
4–5, 7–8** *(2b)*

*R. My soul is thirsting for you,
O Lord my God.*

*You are my God. I worship you.
In my heart, I long for you,
as I would long for a stream
in a scorching desert.*

*R. My soul is thirsting for you,
O Lord my God.*

*I have seen your power
and your glory
in the place of worship.
Your love means more
than life to me,
and I praise you.*

*R. My soul is thirsting for you,
O Lord my God.*

*As long as I live,
I will pray to you.
I will sing joyful praises
and be filled with excitement
like a guest at a banquet.*

*R. My soul is thirsting for you,
O Lord my God.*

*You have helped me,
and I sing happy songs
in the shadow of your wings.
I stay close to you,
and your powerful arm
supports me.*

*R. My soul is thirsting for you,
O Lord my God.*

FIVE

Psalm 95:1 – 2, 3 – 5, 6 – 7 *(8)*

R. *If today you hear God's voice, harden not your hearts.*

Sing joyful songs to the LORD!
Praise the mighty rock
where we are safe.
Come to worship him
with thankful hearts
and songs of praise.

R. *If today you hear God's voice, harden not your hearts.*

The LORD is the greatest God,
king over all other gods.
He holds the deepest part
of the earth in his hands,
and the mountain peaks
belong to him.
The ocean is the LORD's
because he made it,
and with his own hands
he formed the dry land.

R. *If today you hear God's voice, harden not your hearts.*

Bow down and worship
the LORD our Creator!
The LORD is our God,
and we are his people,
the sheep he takes care of
in his own pasture.
Listen to God's voice today!

R. *If today you hear God's voice, harden not your hearts.*

SIX

**Psalm 100:1 – 2, 3,
5** *(3c)*

R. *We are God's people: the sheep of his flock.*

Shout praises to the Lord,
everyone on this earth.
Be joyful and sing
as you come in
to worship the Lord!

R. *We are God's people: the sheep of his flock.*

You know the Lord is God!
He created us,
and we belong to him;
we are his people,
the sheep in his pasture.

R. *We are God's people: the sheep of his flock.*

The Lord is good!
His love and faithfulness
will last forever.

R. *We are God's people: the sheep of his flock.*

SEVEN

**Psalm 103:1 – 2,
8 and 10, 12 – 13
*(8a)***

R. *The Lord is kind and merciful.*

*With all my heart
I praise the LORD,
and with all that I am
I praise his holy name!
With all my heart
I praise the LORD!
I will never forget
how kind he has been.*

R. *The Lord is kind and merciful.*

*The LORD is merciful!
He is kind and patient,
and his love never fails.
He doesn't punish us
as our sins deserve.*

R. *The Lord is kind and merciful.*

*How far has the LORD taken
our sins from us?
Farther than the distance
from east to west!
Just as parents are kind
to their children,
the LORD is kind
to all who worship him.*

R. *The Lord is kind and merciful.*

EIGHT

Psalm 145:1 – 2,
8 – 9, 10 – 11,
13cd – 14 *(see 1)*

R. I will praise your name for ever,
my king and my God.

I will praise you,
my God and King,
and always honor your name.
I will praise you each day
and always honor your name.

R. I will praise your name for ever,
my king and my God.

*You are merciful, L*ORD*!*
You are kind and patient
and always loving.
You are good to everyone,
and you take care
of all your creation.

R. I will praise your name for ever,
my king and my God.

All creation will thank you,
and your loyal people
will praise you.
They will tell about
your marvelous kingdom
and your power.

R. I will praise your name for ever,
my king and my God.

*Our L*ORD*, you keep your word*
and do everything you say.
When someone stumbles or falls,
you give a helping hand.

R. I will praise your name for ever,
my king and my God.

Last Weeks in Ordinary Time

NINE

Psalm 122:1 – 2, R. *Let us go rejoicing to the house of the Lord.*
6 – 7, 8 – 9 *(see 1)*

It made me glad
to hear them say,
"Let's go to the house
of the LORD!"
Jerusalem, we are standing
inside your gates.

R. *Let us go rejoicing to the house of the Lord.*

Jerusalem, we pray
that you will have peace,
and that all will go well
for those who love you.
May there be peace
inside your city walls
and in your palaces.

R. *Let us go rejoicing to the house of the Lord.*

Because of my friends
and my relatives,
I will pray for peace.
And because of the house
of the LORD our God,
I will work for your good.

R. *Let us go rejoicing to the house of the Lord.*

CALENDAR

SUNDAY/FEAST DAY	1993	1994	1995	1996
	Year A	Year B	Year C	Year A
1st Sunday of Advent	Nov. 29, 1992	Nov. 28, 1993	Nov. 27, 1994	Dec. 3, 1995
2nd Sunday of Advent	Dec. 6, 1992	Dec. 5, 1993	Dec. 4, 1994	Dec. 10, 1995
Immaculate Conception, December 8	Tuesday	Wednesday	Thursday	Friday
3rd Sunday of Advent	Dec. 13, 1992	Dec. 12, 1993	Dec. 11, 1994	Dec. 17, 1995
4th Sunday of Advent	Dec. 29, 1992	Dec. 19, 1993	Dec. 18, 1994	Dec. 24, 1995
Christmas, December 25	Friday	Saturday	Sunday	Monday
Holy Family	Dec. 27, 1992	Dec. 26, 1993	Dec. 30, 1994*	Dec. 31, 1995
Mary, Mother of God, January 1	Friday	Saturday	Sunday	Monday
Epiphany	Jan. 3, 1993	Jan. 2, 1994	Jan. 8, 1995	Jan. 7, 1996
Baptism of the Lord	Jan. 10, 1993	Jan. 9, 1994	Jan. 9, 1995*	Jan. 8, 1996*
2nd Sunday in Ordinary Time	Jan. 17	Jan. 16	Jan. 15	Jan. 14
3rd Sunday in Ordinary Time	Jan. 24	Jan. 23	Jan. 22	Jan. 21
4th Sunday in Ordinary Time	Jan. 31	Jan. 30	Jan. 29	Jan. 28
Presentation of the Lord, February 2	Tuesday	Wednesday	Thursday	Friday
5th Sunday in Ordinary Time	Feb. 7	Feb. 6	Feb. 5	Feb. 4
6th Sunday in Ordinary Time	Feb. 14	Feb. 13	Feb. 12	Feb. 11
7th Sunday in Ordinary Time	Feb. 21	■	Feb. 19	Feb. 18
8th Sunday in Ordinary Time	■	■	Feb. 26	■
9th Sunday in Ordinary Time	■	■	■	■
Ash Wednesday	Feb. 24	Feb. 16	Mar. 1	Feb. 21
1st Sunday of Lent	Feb. 28	Feb. 20	Mar. 5	Feb. 25
2nd Sunday of Lent	Mar. 7	Feb. 27	Mar. 12	Mar. 3
3rd Sunday of Lent	Mar. 14	Mar. 6	Mar. 19	Mar. 10
4th Sunday of Lent	Mar. 21	Mar. 13	Mar. 26	Mar. 17
5th Sunday of Lent	Mar. 28	Mar. 20	Apr. 2	Mar. 24
Passion (Palm) Sunday	Apr. 4	Mar. 27	Apr. 9	Mar. 31
• Joseph, Husband of Mary, March 19	Friday	Saturday	Mar. 20†	Tuesday
• Annunciation, March 25	Thursday	Friday	Saturday	Monday
Holy Thursday	Apr. 8	Mar. 31	Apr. 13	Apr. 4
Good Friday	Apr. 9	Apr. 1	Apr. 14	Apr. 5
Easter Sunday	Apr. 11	Apr. 3	Apr. 16	Apr. 7
2nd Sunday of Easter	Apr. 18	Apr. 10	Apr. 23	Apr. 14
3rd Sunday of Easter	Apr. 25	Apr. 17	Apr. 30	Apr. 21
4th Sunday of Easter	May 2	Apr. 24	May 7	Apr. 28
5th Sunday of Easter	May 9	May 1	May 14	May 5

* *This feast is celebrated this year on a weekday.*   † *This solemnity has been transferred to this date.*

SUNDAY/FEAST DAY	1993	1994	1995	1996
	Year A	Year B	Year C	Year A
6th Sunday of Easter	May 16	May 8	May 21	May 12
Ascension	May 20	May 12	May 25	May 16
7th Sunday of Easter	May 23	May 15	May 28	May 19
Pentecost	May 30	May 22	June 4	May 26
Trinity Sunday	June 6	May 29	June 11	June 2
Body and Blood of Christ	June 13	June 5	June 18	June 9
Sacred Heart	June 18	June 10	June 23	June 14
9th Sunday in Ordinary Time	■	■	■	■
10th Sunday in Ordinary Time	■	■	■	■
11th Sunday in Ordinary Time	■	June 12	■	June 16
12th Sunday in Ordinary Time	June 20	June 19	June 25	June 23
Birth of John the Baptist, June 24	Thursday	Friday	Saturday	Monday
13th Sunday in Ordinary Time	June 27	June 26	July 2	June 30
Peter and Paul, Apostles, June 29	Tuesday	Wednesday	Thursday	Saturday
14th Sunday in Ordinary Time	July 4	July 3	July 9	July 7
15th Sunday in Ordinary Time	July 11	July 10	July 16	July 14
16th Sunday in Ordinary Time	July 18	July 17	July 23	July 21
17th Sunday in Ordinary Time	July 25	July 24	July 30	July 28
18th Sunday in Ordinary Time	Aug. 1	July 31	■	Aug. 4
Transfiguration, August 6	Friday	Saturday	Sunday	Tuesday
19th Sunday in Ordinary Time	Aug. 8	Aug. 7	Aug. 13	Aug. 11
Assumption, August 15	Sunday	Monday	Tuesday	Thursday
20th Sunday in Ordinary Time	■	Aug. 14	Aug. 20	Aug. 18
21st Sunday in Ordinary Time	Aug. 22	Aug. 21	Aug. 27	Aug. 25
22nd Sunday in Ordinary Time	Aug. 29	Aug. 28	Sept. 3	Sept. 1
23rd Sunday in Ordinary Time	Sept. 5	Sept. 4	Sept. 10	Sept. 8
Triumph of the Cross, September 14	Tuesday	Wednesday	Thursday	Saturday
24th Sunday in Ordinary Time	Sept. 12	Sept. 11	Sept. 17	Sept. 15
25th Sunday in Ordinary Time	Sept. 19	Sept. 18	Sept. 24	Sept. 22
26th Sunday in Ordinary Time	Sept. 26	Sept. 25	Oct. 1	Sept. 29
27th Sunday in Ordinary Time	Oct. 3	Oct. 2	Oct. 8	Oct. 6
28th Sunday in Ordinary Time	Oct. 10	Oct. 9	Oct. 15	Oct. 13
29th Sunday in Ordinary Time	Oct. 17	Oct. 16	Oct. 22	Oct. 20
30th Sunday in Ordinary Time	Oct. 24	Oct. 23	Oct. 29	Oct. 27
31st Sunday in Ordinary Time	Oct. 31	Oct. 30	Nov. 5	Nov. 3
All Saints, November 1	Monday	Tuesday	Wednesday	Friday
All Souls, November 2	Tuesday	Wednesday	Thursday	Saturday
32nd Sunday in Ordinary Time	Nov. 7	Nov. 6	Nov. 12	Nov. 10
Dedication of St. John Lateran, November 9	Tuesday	Wednesday	Thursday	Saturday
33rd Sunday in Ordinary Time	Nov. 14	Nov. 13	Nov. 19	Nov. 17
Christ the King	Nov. 21	Nov. 20	Nov. 26	Nov. 24

SUNDAY/FEAST DAY	1997	1998	1999	2000
	Year B	Year C	Year A	Year B
1st Sunday of Advent	Dec. 1, 1996	Nov. 30, 1997	Nov. 29, 1998	Nov 28, 1999
2nd Sunday of Advent	Dec. 8, 1996	Dec. 7, 1997	Dec. 6, 1998	Dec. 5, 1999
Immaculate Conception, December 8	Dec. 9, 1996†	Monday	Tuesday	Wednesday
3rd Sunday of Advent	Dec. 15, 1996	Dec. 14, 1997	Dec. 13, 1998	Dec. 12, 1999
4th Sunday of Advent	Dec. 22, 1996	Dec. 21, 1997	Dec. 20, 1998	Dec. 19, 1999
Christmas, December 25	Wednesday	Thursday	Friday	Saturday
Holy Family	Dec. 29, 1996	Dec. 28, 1997	Dec. 27, 1998	Dec. 26, 1999
Mary, Mother of God, January 1	Wednesday	Thursday	Friday	Saturday
Epiphany	Jan. 5, 1997	Jan. 4, 1998	Jan. 3, 1999	Jan. 2, 2000
Baptism of the Lord	Jan. 12, 1997	Jan. 11, 1998	Jan. 10, 1999	Jan. 9, 2000
2nd Sunday in Ordinary Time	Jan. 19	Jan. 18	Jan. 17	Jan. 16
3rd Sunday in Ordinary Time	Jan. 26	Jan. 25	Jan. 24	Jan. 23
4th Sunday in Ordinary Time	■	Feb. 1	Jan. 31	Jan. 30
Presentation of the Lord, February 2	Sunday	Monday	Tuesday	Wednesday
5th Sunday in Ordinary Time	Feb. 9	Feb. 8	Feb. 7	Feb. 6
6th Sunday in Ordinary Time	■	Feb. 15	Feb. 14	Feb. 13
7th Sunday in Ordinary Time	■	Feb. 22	■	Feb. 20
8th Sunday in Ordinary Time	■	■	■	Feb. 27
9th Sunday in Ordinary Time	■	■	■	Mar. 5
Ash Wednesday	Feb. 12	Feb. 25	Feb. 17	Mar. 8
1st Sunday of Lent	Feb. 16	Mar. 1	Feb. 21	Mar. 12
2nd Sunday of Lent	Feb. 23	Mar. 8	Feb. 28	Mar. 19
3rd Sunday of Lent	Mar. 2	Mar. 15	Mar. 7	Mar. 26
4th Sunday of Lent	Mar. 9	Mar. 22	Mar. 14	Apr. 2
5th Sunday of Lent	Mar. 16	Mar. 29	Mar. 21	Apr. 9
Passion (Palm) Sunday	Mar. 23	Apr. 5	Mar 28	Apr. 16
• Joseph, Husband of Mary, March 19	Tuesday	Thursday	Friday	Mar. 20†
• Annunciation, March 25	Apr. 7†	Wednesday	Thursday	Saturday
Holy Thursday	Mar. 27	Apr. 9	Apr. 1	Apr. 20
Good Friday	Mar. 28	Apr. 10	Apr. 2	Apr. 21
Easter Sunday	Mar. 30	Apr. 12	Apr. 4	Apr. 23
2nd Sunday of Easter	Apr. 6	Apr. 19	Apr. 11	Apr. 30
3rd Sunday of Easter	Apr. 13	Apr. 26	Apr. 18	May 7
4th Sunday of Easter	Apr. 20	May 3	Apr. 25	May 14
5th Sunday of Easter	Apr. 27	May 10	May 2	May 21

† This solemnity has been transferred to this date.

SUNDAY/FEAST DAY	1997	1998	1999	2000
	Year B	Year C	Year A	Year B
6th Sunday of Easter	May 4	May 17	May 9	May 28
Ascension	May 8	May 21	May 13	June 1
7th Sunday of Easter	May 11	May 24	May 16	June 4
Pentecost	May 18	May 31	May 23	June 11
Trinity Sunday	May 25	June 7	May 30	June 18
Body and Blood of Christ	June 1	June 14	June 6	June 25
Sacred Heart	June 6	June 19	June 11	June 30
9th Sunday in Ordinary Time	■	■	■	■
10th Sunday in Ordinary Time	June 8	■	■	■
11th Sunday in Ordinary Time	June 15	■	June 13	■
12th Sunday in Ordinary Time	June 22	June 21	June 20	■
Birth of John the Baptist, June 24	Tuesday	Wednesday	Thursday	Saturday
13th Sunday in Ordinary Time	■	June 28	June 27	July 2
Peter and Paul, Apostles, June 29	Sunday	Monday	Tuesday	Thursday
14th Sunday in Ordinary Time	July 6	July 5	July 4	July 9
15th Sunday in Ordinary Time	July 13	July 12	July 11	July 16
16th Sunday in Ordinary Time	July 20	July 19	July 18	July 23
17th Sunday in Ordinary Time	July 27	July 26	July 25	July 30
18th Sunday in Ordinary Time	Aug. 3	Aug. 2	Aug. 1	■
Transfiguration, August 6	Wednesday	Thursday	Friday	Sunday
19th Sunday in Ordinary Time	Aug. 10	Aug. 9	Aug. 8	Aug. 13
Assumption, August 15	Friday	Saturday	Sunday	Tuesday
20th Sunday in Ordinary Time	Aug. 17	Aug. 16	■	Aug. 20
21st Sunday in Ordinary Time	Aug. 24	Aug. 23	Aug. 22	Aug. 27
22nd Sunday in Ordinary Time	Aug. 31	Aug. 30	Aug. 29	Sept. 3
23rd Sunday in Ordinary Time	Sept. 7	Sept. 6	Sept. 5	Sept. 10
Triumph of the Cross, September 14	Sunday	Monday	Tuesday	Thursday
24th Sunday in Ordinary Time	■	Sept. 13	Sept. 12	Sept. 17
25th Sunday in Ordinary Time	Sept. 21	Sept. 20	Sept. 19	Sept. 24
26th Sunday in Ordinary Time	Sept. 28	Sept. 27	Sept. 26	Oct. 1
27th Sunday in Ordinary Time	Oct. 5	Oct. 4	Oct. 3	Oct. 8
28th Sunday in Ordinary Time	Oct. 12	Oct. 11	Oct. 10	Oct. 15
29th Sunday in Ordinary Time	Oct. 19	Oct. 18	Oct. 17	Oct. 22
30th Sunday in Ordinary Time	Oct. 26	Oct. 25	Oct. 24	Oct. 29
31st Sunday in Ordinary Time	■	■	Oct. 31	Nov. 5
All Saints, November 1	Saturday	Sunday	Monday	Wednesday
All Souls, November 2	Sunday	Monday	Tuesday	Thursday
32nd Sunday in Ordinary Time	■	Nov. 8	Nov. 7	Nov. 12
Dedication of St. John Lateran, November 9	Sunday	Monday	Tuesday	Thursday
33rd Sunday in Ordinary Time	Nov. 16	Nov. 15	Nov. 14	Nov. 19
Christ the King	Nov. 23	Nov. 22	Nov. 21	Nov. 26

SUNDAY/FEAST DAY	2001	2002	2003	2004
	Year C	Year A	Year B	Year C
1st Sunday of Advent	Dec. 3, 2000	Dec. 2, 2001	Dec. 1, 2002	Nov. 30, 2003
2nd Sunday of Advent	Dec. 10, 2000	Dec. 9, 2001	Dec. 8, 2002	Dec. 7, 2003
Immaculate Conception, December 8	Friday	Saturday	Dec. 9, 2002†	Monday
3rd Sunday of Advent	Dec. 17, 2000	Dec. 16, 2001	Dec. 15, 2002	Dec. 14, 2003
4th Sunday of Advent	Dec. 24, 2000	Dec. 23, 2001	Dec. 22, 2002	Dec. 21, 2003
Christmas, December 25	Monday	Tuesday	Wednesday	Thursday
Holy Family	Dec. 31, 2000	Dec. 30, 2001	Dec. 29, 2002	Dec. 28, 2003
Mary, Mother of God, January 1	Monday	Tuesday	Wednesday	Thursday
Epiphany	Jan. 7, 2001	Jan. 6, 2002	Jan. 5, 2003	Jan. 4, 2004
Baptism of the Lord	Jan. 8, 2001*	Jan. 13, 2002	Jan. 12, 2003	Jan. 11, 2004
2nd Sunday in Ordinary Time	Jan. 14	Jan. 20	Jan. 19	Jan. 18
3rd Sunday in Ordinary Time	Jan. 21	Jan. 27	Jan. 26	Jan. 25
4th Sunday in Ordinary Time	Jan. 28	Feb. 3	■	Feb. 1
Presentation of the Lord, February 2	Friday	Saturday	Sunday	Monday
5th Sunday in Ordinary Time	Feb. 4	Feb. 10	Feb. 9	Feb. 8
6th Sunday in Ordinary Time	Feb. 11	■	Feb. 16	Feb. 15
7th Sunday in Ordinary Time	Feb. 18	■	Feb. 23	Feb. 22
8th Sunday in Ordinary Time	Feb. 25	■	Mar. 2	■
9th Sunday in Ordinary Time	■	■	■	■
Ash Wednesday	Feb. 28	Feb. 13	Mar. 5	Feb. 25
1st Sunday of Lent	Mar. 4	Feb. 17	Mar. 9	Feb. 29
2nd Sunday of Lent	Mar. 11	Feb. 24	Mar. 16	Mar. 7
3rd Sunday of Lent	Mar. 18	Mar. 3	Mar. 23	Mar. 14
4th Sunday of Lent	Mar. 25	Mar. 10	Mar. 30	Mar. 21
5th Sunday of Lent	Apr. 1	Mar. 17	Apr. 6	Mar. 28
Passion (Palm) Sunday	Apr. 8	Mar. 24	Apr. 13	Apr. 4
• Joseph, Husband of Mary, March 19	Monday	Tuesday	Wednesday	Friday
• Annunciation, March 25	Mar. 26†	Apr. 8†	Tuesday	Thursday
Holy Thursday	Apr. 12	Mar. 28	Apr. 17	Apr. 8
Good Friday	Apr. 13	Mar. 29	Apr. 18	Apr. 9
Easter Sunday	Apr. 15	Mar. 31	Apr. 20	Apr. 11
2nd Sunday of Easter	Apr. 22	Apr. 7	Apr. 27	Apr. 18
3rd Sunday of Easter	Apr. 29	Apr. 14	May 4	Apr. 25
4th Sunday of Easter	May 6	Apr. 21	May 11	May 2
5th Sunday of Easter	May 13	Apr. 28	May 18	May 9

* *This feast is celebrated this year on a weekday.*   † *This solemnity has been transferred to this date.*

SUNDAY/FEAST DAY	2001	2002	2003	2004
	Year C	Year A	Year B	Year C
6th Sunday of Easter	May 20	May 5	May 25	May 16
Ascension	May 24	May 9	May 29	May 20
7th Sunday of Easter	May 27	May 12	June 1	May 23
Pentecost	June 3	May 19	June 8	May 30
Trinity Sunday	June 10	May 26	June 15	June 6
Body and Blood of Christ	June 17	June 2	June 22	June 13
Sacred Heart	June 22	June 7	June 27	June 18
9th Sunday in Ordinary Time	■	■	■	■
10th Sunday in Ordinary Time	■	June 9	■	■
11th Sunday in Ordinary Time	■	June 16	■	■
12th Sunday in Ordinary Time	■	June 23	■	June 20
Birth of John the Baptist, June 24	Sunday	Monday	Tuesday	Thursday
13th Sunday in Ordinary Time	July 1	June 30	■	June 27
Peter and Paul, Apostles, June 29	Friday	Saturday	Sunday	Tuesday
14th Sunday in Ordinary Time	July 8	July 7	July 6	July 4
15th Sunday in Ordinary Time	July 15	July 14	July 13	July 11
16th Sunday in Ordinary Time	July 22	July 21	July 20	July 18
17th Sunday in Ordinary Time	July 29	July 28	July 27	July 25
18th Sunday in Ordinary Time	Aug. 5	Aug. 4	Aug. 3	Aug. 1
Transfiguration, August 6	Monday	Tuesday	Wednesday	Friday
19th Sunday in Ordinary Time	Aug. 12	Aug. 11	Aug. 10	Aug. 8
Assumption, August 15	Wednesday	Thursday	Friday	Sunday
20th Sunday in Ordinary Time	Aug. 19	Aug. 18	Aug. 17	■
21st Sunday in Ordinary Time	Aug. 26	Aug. 25	Aug. 24	Aug. 22
22nd Sunday in Ordinary Time	Sept. 2	Sept. 1	Aug. 31	Aug. 29
23rd Sunday in Ordinary Time	Sept. 9	Sept. 8	Sept. 7	Sept. 5
Triumph of the Cross, September 14	Friday	Saturday	Sunday	Tuesday
24th Sunday in Ordinary Time	Sept. 16	Sept. 15	■	Sept. 12
25th Sunday in Ordinary Time	Sept. 23	Sept. 22	Sept. 21	Sept. 19
26th Sunday in Ordinary Time	Sept. 30	Sept. 29	Sept. 28	Sept. 26
27th Sunday in Ordinary Time	Oct. 7	Oct. 6	Oct. 5	Oct. 3
28th Sunday in Ordinary Time	Oct. 14	Oct. 13	Oct. 12	Oct. 10
29th Sunday in Ordinary Time	Oct. 21	Oct. 20	Oct. 19	Oct. 17
30th Sunday in Ordinary Time	Oct. 28	Oct. 27	Oct. 26	Oct. 24
31st Sunday in Ordinary Time	Nov. 4	Nov. 3	■	Oct. 31
All Saints, November 1	Thursday	Friday	Saturday	Monday
All Souls, November 2	Friday	Saturday	Sunday	Tuesday
32nd Sunday in Ordinary Time	Nov. 11	Nov. 10	■	Nov. 7
Dedication of St. John Lateran, November 9	Friday	Saturday	Sunday	Tuesday
33rd Sunday in Ordinary Time	Nov. 18	Nov. 17	Nov. 16	Nov. 14
Christ the King	Nov. 25	Nov. 24	Nov. 23	Nov. 21

CALENDAR

SUNDAY/FEAST DAY	2005 Year A	2006 Year B	2007 Year C	2008 Year A
1st Sunday of Advent	Nov. 28, 2004	Nov. 27, 2005	Dec. 3, 2006	Dec. 2, 2007
2nd Sunday of Advent	Dec. 5, 2004	Dec. 4, 2005	Dec. 10, 2006	Dec. 9, 2007
Immaculate Conception, December 8	Wednesday	Thursday	Friday	Saturday
3rd Sunday of Advent	Dec. 12, 2004	Dec. 11, 2005	Dec. 17, 2006	Dec. 16, 2007
4th Sunday of Advent	Dec. 19, 2004	Dec. 18, 2005	Dec. 24, 2006	Dec. 23, 2007
Christmas, December 25	Saturday	Sunday	Monday	Tuesday
Holy Family	Dec. 26, 2004	Dec. 30, 2005*	Dec. 31, 2006	Dec. 30, 2007
Mary, Mother of God, January 1	Saturday	Sunday	Monday	Tuesday
Epiphany	Jan. 2, 2005	Jan. 8, 2006	Jan. 7, 2007	Jan. 6, 2008
Baptism of the Lord	Jan. 9, 2005	Jan. 9, 2006*	Jan. 8, 2007*	Jan. 13, 2008
2nd Sunday in Ordinary Time	Jan. 16	Jan. 15	Jan. 14	Jan. 20
3rd Sunday in Ordinary Time	Jan. 23	Jan. 22	Jan. 21	Jan. 27
4th Sunday in Ordinary Time	Jan. 30	Jan. 29	Jan. 28	Feb. 3
Presentation of the Lord, February 2	Wednesday	Thursday	Friday	Saturday
5th Sunday in Ordinary Time	Feb. 6	Feb. 5	Feb. 4	■
6th Sunday in Ordinary Time	■	Feb. 12	Feb. 11	■
7th Sunday in Ordinary Time	■	Feb. 19	Feb. 18	■
8th Sunday in Ordinary Time	■	Feb. 26	■	■
9th Sunday in Ordinary Time	■	■	■	■
Ash Wednesday	Feb. 9	Mar. 1	Feb. 21	Feb. 6
1st Sunday of Lent	Feb. 13	Mar. 5	Feb. 25	Feb. 10
2nd Sunday of Lent	Feb. 20	Mar. 12	Mar. 4	Feb. 17
3rd Sunday of Lent	Feb. 27	Mar. 19	Mar. 11	Feb. 24
4th Sunday of Lent	Mar. 6	Mar. 26	Mar. 18	Mar. 2
5th Sunday of Lent	Mar. 13	Apr. 2	Mar. 25	Mar. 9
Passion (Palm) Sunday	Mar. 20	Apr. 9	Apr. 1	Mar. 16
• Joseph, Husband of Mary, March 19	Saturday	Mar. 20†	Monday	Mar. 31†
• Annunciation, March 25	Apr. 4†	Saturday	Mar. 26†	Apr. 1†
Holy Thursday	Mar. 24	Apr. 13	Apr. 5	Mar. 20
Good Friday	Mar. 25	Apr. 14	Apr. 6	Mar. 21
Easter Sunday	Mar. 27	Apr. 16	Apr. 8	Mar. 23
2nd Sunday of Easter	Apr. 3	Apr. 23	Apr. 15	Mar. 30
3rd Sunday of Easter	Apr. 10	Apr. 30	Apr. 22	Apr. 6
4th Sunday of Easter	Apr. 17	May 7	Apr. 29	Apr. 13
5th Sunday of Easter	Apr. 24	May 14	May 6	Apr. 20

* *This feast is celebrated this year on a weekday.*   † *This solemnity has been transferred to this date.*

SUNDAY/FEAST DAY	2005	2006	2007	2008
	Year A	Year B	Year C	Year A
6th Sunday of Easter	May 1	May 21	May 13	Apr. 27
Ascension	May 5	May 25	May 17	May 1
7th Sunday of Easter	May 8	May 28	May 20	May 4
Pentecost	May 15	June 4	May 27	May 11
Trinity Sunday	May 22	June 11	June 3	May 18
Body and Blood of Christ	May 29	June 18	June 10	May 25
Sacred Heart	June 3	June 23	June 15	May 30
9th Sunday in Ordinary Time	■	■	■	June 1
10th Sunday in Ordinary Time	June 5	■	■	June 8
11th Sunday in Ordinary Time	June 12	■	June 17	June 15
12th Sunday in Ordinary Time	June 19	June 25	■	June 22
Birth of John the Baptist, June 24	Friday	Saturday	Sunday	Tuesday
13th Sunday in Ordinary Time	June 26	July 2	July 1	■
Peter and Paul, Apostles, June 29	Wednesday	Thursday	Friday	Sunday
14th Sunday in Ordinary Time	July 3	July 9	July 8	July 6
15th Sunday in Ordinary Time	July 10	July 16	July 15	July 13
16th Sunday in Ordinary Time	July 17	July 23	July 22	July 20
17th Sunday in Ordinary Time	July 24	July 30	July 29	July 27
18th Sunday in Ordinary Time	July 31	■	Aug. 5	Aug. 3
Transfiguration, August 6	Saturday	Sunday	Monday	Wednesday
19th Sunday in Ordinary Time	Aug. 7	Aug. 13	Aug. 12	Aug. 10
Assumption, August 15	Monday	Tuesday	Wednesday	Friday
20th Sunday in Ordinary Time	Aug. 14	Aug. 20	Aug. 19	Aug. 17
21st Sunday in Ordinary Time	Aug. 21	Aug. 27	Aug. 26	Aug. 24
22nd Sunday in Ordinary Time	Aug. 28	Sept. 3	Sept. 2	Aug. 31
23rd Sunday in Ordinary Time	Sept. 4	Sept. 10	Sept. 9	Sept. 7
Triumph of the Cross, September 14	Wednesday	Thursday	Friday	Sunday
24th Sunday in Ordinary Time	Sept. 11	Sept. 17	Sept. 16	■
25th Sunday in Ordinary Time	Sept. 18	Sept. 24	Sept. 23	Sept. 21
26th Sunday in Ordinary Time	Sept. 25	Oct. 1	Sept. 30	Sept. 28
27th Sunday in Ordinary Time	Oct. 2	Oct. 8	Oct. 7	Oct. 5
28th Sunday in Ordinary Time	Oct. 9	Oct. 15	Oct. 14	Oct. 12
29th Sunday in Ordinary Time	Oct. 16	Oct. 22	Oct. 21	Oct. 19
30th Sunday in Ordinary Time	Oct. 23	Oct. 29	Oct. 28	Oct. 26
31st Sunday in Ordinary Time	Oct. 30	Nov. 5	Nov. 4	■
All Saints, November 1	Tuesday	Wednesday	Thursday	Saturday
All Souls, November 2	Wednesday	Thursday	Friday	Sunday
32nd Sunday in Ordinary Time	Nov. 6	Nov. 12	Nov. 11	■
Dedication of St. John Lateran, November 9	Wednesday	Thursday	Friday	Sunday
33rd Sunday in Ordinary Time	Nov. 13	Nov. 19	Nov. 18	Nov. 16
Christ the King	Nov. 20	Nov. 26	Nov. 25	Nov. 23

SUNDAY/FEAST DAY	2009	2010	2011	2012
	Year B	Year C	Year A	Year B
1st Sunday of Advent	Nov. 30, 2008	Nov. 29, 2009	Nov. 28, 2010	Nov. 27, 2011
2nd Sunday of Advent	Dec. 7, 2008	Dec. 6, 2009	Dec. 5, 2010	Dec. 4, 2011
Immaculate Conception, December 8	Monday	Tuesday	Wednesday	Thursday
3rd Sunday of Advent	Dec. 14, 2008	Dec. 13, 2009	Dec. 12, 2010	Dec. 11, 2011
4th Sunday of Advent	Dec. 21, 2008	Dec. 20, 2009	Dec. 19, 2010	Dec. 18, 2011
Christmas, Dec. 25	Thursday	Friday	Saturday	Sunday
Holy Family	Dec. 28, 2008	Dec. 27, 2009	Dec. 26, 2010	Dec. 30, 2011*
Mary, Mother of God, January 1	Thursday	Friday	Saturday	Sunday
Epiphany	Jan. 4, 2009	Jan. 3, 2010	Jan. 2, 2011	Jan. 8, 2012
Baptism of the Lord	Jan. 11, 2009	Jan. 10, 2010	Jan. 9, 2011	Jan. 9, 2012*
2nd Sunday in Ordinary Time	Jan. 18	Jan. 17	Jan. 16	Jan. 15
3rd Sunday in Ordinary Time	Jan. 25	Jan. 24	Jan. 23	Jan. 22
4th Sunday in Ordinary Time	Feb. 1	Jan. 31	Jan. 30	Jan. 29
Presentation of the Lord, February 2	Monday	Tuesday	Wednesday	Thursday
5th Sunday in Ordinary Time	Feb. 8	Feb. 7	Feb. 6	Feb. 5
6th Sunday in Ordinary Time	Feb. 15	Feb. 14	Feb. 13	Feb. 12
7th Sunday in Ordinary Time	Feb. 22	■	Feb. 20	Feb. 19
8th Sunday in Ordinary Time	■	■	Feb. 27	■
9th Sunday in Ordinary Time	■	■	Mar. 6	■
Ash Wednesday	Feb. 25	Feb. 17	Mar. 9	Feb. 22
1st Sunday of Lent	Mar. 1	Feb. 21	Mar. 13	Feb. 26
2nd Sunday of Lent	Mar. 8	Feb. 28	Mar. 20	Mar. 4
3rd Sunday of Lent	Mar. 15	Mar. 7	Mar. 27	Mar. 11
4th Sunday of Lent	Mar. 22	Mar. 14	Apr. 3	Mar. 18
5th Sunday of Lent	Mar. 29	Mar. 21	Apr. 10	Mar. 25
Passion (Palm) Sunday	Apr. 5	Mar. 28	Apr. 17	Apr. 1
• Joseph, Husband of Mary, March 19	Thursday	Friday	Saturday	Monday
• Annunciation, March 25	Wednesday	Thursday	Friday	Mar. 26†
Holy Thursday	Apr. 9	Apr. 1	Apr. 21	Apr. 5
Good Friday	Apr. 10	Apr. 2	Apr. 22	Apr. 6
Easter Sunday	Apr. 12	Apr. 4	Apr. 24	Apr. 8
2nd Sunday of Easter	Apr. 19	Apr. 11	May 1	Apr. 15
3rd Sunday of Easter	Apr. 26	Apr. 18	May 8	Apr. 22
4th Sunday of Easter	May 3	Apr. 25	May 15	Apr. 29
5th Sunday of Easter	May 10	May 2	May 22	May 6

* This feast is celebrated this year on a weekday.   † This solemnity has been transferred to this date.

CALENDAR

SUNDAY/FEAST DAY	2009	2010	2011	2012
	Year B	Year C	Year A	Year B
6th Sunday of Easter	May 17	May 9	May 29	May 13
Ascension	May 21	May 13	June 2	May 17
7th Sunday of Easter	May 24	May 16	June 5	May 20
Pentecost	May 31	May 23	June 12	May 27
Trinity Sunday	June 7	May 30	June 19	June 3
Body and Blood of Christ	June 14	June 6	June 26	June 10
Sacred Heart	June 19	June 11	July 1	June 15
9th Sunday in Ordinary Time	■	■	■	■
10th Sunday in Ordinary Time	■	■	■	■
11th Sunday in Ordinary Time	■	June 13	■	June 17
12th Sunday in Ordinary Time	June 21	June 20	■	■
Birth of John the Baptist, June 24	Wednesday	Thursday	Friday	Sunday
13th Sunday in Ordinary Time	June 28	June 27	■	July 1
Peter and Paul, Apostles, June 29	Monday	Tuesday	Wednesday	Friday
14th Sunday in Ordinary Time	July 5	July 4	July 3	July 8
15th Sunday in Ordinary Time	July 12	July 11	July 10	July 15
16th Sunday in Ordinary Time	July 19	July 18	July 17	July 22
17th Sunday in Ordinary Time	July 26	July 25	July 24	July 29
18th Sunday in Ordinary Time	Aug. 2	Aug. 1	July 31	Aug. 5
Transfiguration, August 6	Thursday	Friday	Saturday	Monday
19th Sunday in Ordinary Time	Aug. 9	Aug. 8	Aug. 7	Aug. 12
Assumption, August 15	Saturday	Sunday	Monday	Wednesday
20th Sunday in Ordinary Time	Aug. 16	■	Aug. 14	Aug. 19
21st Sunday in Ordinary Time	Aug. 23	Aug. 22	Aug. 21	Aug. 26
22nd Sunday in Ordinary Time	Aug. 30	Aug. 29	Aug. 28	Sept. 2
23rd Sunday in Ordinary Time	Sept. 6	Sept. 5	Sept. 4	Sept. 9
Triumph of the Cross, September 14	Monday	Tuesday	Wednesday	Friday
24th Sunday in Ordinary Time	Sept. 13	Sept. 12	Sept. 11	Sept. 16
25th Sunday in Ordinary Time	Sept. 20	Sept. 19	Sept. 18	Sept. 23
26th Sunday in Ordinary Time	Sept. 27	Sept. 26	Sept. 25	Sept. 30
27th Sunday in Ordinary Time	Oct. 4	Oct. 3	Oct. 2	Oct. 7
28th Sunday in Ordinary Time	Oct. 11	Oct. 10	Oct. 9	Oct. 14
29th Sunday in Ordinary Time	Oct. 18	Oct. 17	Oct. 16	Oct. 21
30th Sunday in Ordinary Time	Oct. 25	Oct. 24	Oct. 23	Oct. 28
31st Sunday in Ordinary Time	■	Oct. 31	Oct. 30	Nov. 4
All Saints, November 1	Sunday	Monday	Tuesday	Thursday
All Souls, November 2	Monday	Tuesday	Wednesday	Friday
32nd Sunday in Ordinary Time	Nov. 8	Nov. 7	Nov. 6	Nov. 11
Dedication of St. John Lateran, November 9	Monday	Tuesday	Wednesday	Friday
33rd Sunday in Ordinary Time	Nov. 15	Nov. 14	Nov. 13	Nov. 18
Christ the King	Nov. 22	Nov. 21	Nov. 20	Nov. 25

INDEX OF READINGS

The numbers on this chart refer to sections, not to pages.

Reading	A	B	C	W
Genesis				
1:11 – 12				518
1:26 — 2:3				288
2:7 – 9; 3:1 – 7	18			
2:18 – 24		135		
3:9 – 15		84		
3:9 – 15, 20				429
9:8 – 15		19		
12:1 – 4a	21			
14:18 – 20			163	
18:1 – 10a			103	
18:20 – 32			106	
50:15 – 21				180
Exodus				
3:1 – 6, 9 – 12				505
3:1 – 8a, 13 – 15			26	
16:2 – 4, 12 – 15		108		
17:3 – 7	24			
19:1 – 6a	86			
20:1 – 3, 7 – 8, 12 – 17		25		
23:20 – 21a				384
24:3 – 8		162		
34:4b – 6, 8 – 9	158			
Leviticus				
19:1 – 2, 17 – 18	74			
Numbers				
6:22 – 27	15	15	15	
11:25 – 29		132		
21:4b – 9				370
Deuteronomy				
4:1 – 2, 6 – 8		120		
4:39 – 40		159		
5:12 – 15		81		
6:2 – 6		147		
7:6 – 11	164			
8:2 – 3, 14b – 16a	161			
8:7 – 10				518
10:12 – 14				182
11:18, 26 – 28	80			
18:18 – 19		66		
26:4 – 10			20	
30:10 – 14			100	
Joshua				
24:1 – 2a, 15 – 17, 18b		117		
1 Samuel				
3:1 – 10				505
3:4 – 10, 19		60		
1 Samuel (continued)				
16:1b, 6 – 7, 10 – 13a	27			
26:2, 7 – 9, 12 – 13, 22 – 23			76	
2 Samuel				
5:1 – 3			157	
7:4 – 5a, 12 – 14a, 16				272
12:7 – 10, 13 – 14			88	
1 Kings				
3:5, 7 – 12	104			
3:11 – 14				465
8:41 – 43			82	
17:10 – 16		150		
17:17 – 24			85	
19:4 – 8		111		
19:9a, 11 – 13a	110			
19:16b, 19 – 21			94	
2 Kings				
4:8 – 11, 14 – 16a	92			
4:42 – 44		105		
5:14 – 17			139	
Nehemiah				
8:1 – 4a, 5 – 6, 8 – 10			64	
2 Maccabees				
7:1, 20 – 23				456
7:1 – 2, 9 – 14			151	
Job				
7:1 – 4, 6 – 7		69		
38:1, 8 – 11		90		
Proverbs				
8:22 – 31			160	
9:1 – 6		114		
Wisdom				
1:13 – 15; 2:23 – 24a		93		
6:12 – 16	149			
7:7 – 11		138		
9:16c – 18			124	
11:22 — 12:1			148	
12:13, 16 – 19	101			
Sirach				
3:2 – 6	14	14	14	
3:17 – 18, 20			121	
15:15 – 20	71			
27:6 – 7			79	
28:2 – 5, 6b – 7	125			

The numbers on this chart refer to sections, not to pages.

Reading	A	B	C	W	Reading	A	B	C	W
Sirach (continued)					**Jeremiah**				
35:12b – 14, 16 – 17			145		1:4 – 5, 17ab, 18 – 19			67	
50:22 – 24				501	1:4 – 8				213
					1:4 – 8				316
Isaiah					1:4 – 9				505
2:1 – 5	1				17:7 – 8			73	
5:1 – 7	134				20:7 – 9	119			
6:1 – 2a, 3 – 8			70		20:10 – 12a, 13	89			
9:2 – 3a, 6 – 7a				447	23:3 – 6		102		
9:2 – 4	62				31:7 – 9		144		
9:2 – 4, 6 – 7	13	13	13		31:31 – 34		31		
11:1b, 5 – 9				224	31:33				222
11:1 – 4a, 5 – 6, 9b	4				33:14 – 16			3	
12:4b – 5				179	38:4 – 6, 8 – 10			115	
25:6 – 7, 9				201					
25:6, 9				229	**Lamentations**				
25:6a, 7 – 9				531	3:22 – 25				183
25:6 – 10a	137								
30:18				210	**Baruch**				
30:19 – 20, 23 – 24, 26				205	5:1 – 5, 7			6	
30:19, 23 – 24, 26				173					
30:19b – 21				172	**Ezekiel**				
32:15 – 20				513	2:2 – 5		96		
35:1 – 2, 5 – 6ab, 10	7				17:22 – 24		87		
35:4 – 7a		123			18:25 – 28	131			
40:3 – 5		5			33:7 – 9	122			
40:10 – 11				218	34:11 – 15				218
40:25 – 26, 29 – 31				174	34:11 – 16abce			166	461
41:10				207	34:11 – 12, 14 – 16abce	155			
41:14				204	36:24 – 28				474
42:1 – 2, 4, 6 – 7	17	17	17		36:24 – 28				479
42:16				208	36:24 – 28				509
43:1 – 3a, 5				211	37:12 – 14		30		
43:18 – 21			32		37:21 – 22, 24				184
43:22 – 25		75							
45:1, 4 – 6	140				**Daniel**				
46:4				197	7:13 – 14		156		
49:3, 5 – 6	59				12:1 – 3		153		
49:14 – 15	77								
50:4 – 8a		126			**Hosea**				
50:6 – 7	33	34	35		2:16b, 17b, 21 – 22		78		
55:1 – 3	107				6:3 – 6	83			
55:6 – 9	128				11:1, 3 – 4, 8c – 9		165		
55:10 – 11	98			203	11:3 – 4				221
56:1, 6 – 7	113			442					
58:6 – 9				176	**Joel**				
58:7 – 10	68				3:1 – 3a				479
60:1 – 6	16	16	16						
61:1 – 2		8			**Amos**				
62:1 – 3			61		7:10 – 15		99		
63:7				496					
66:10 – 14c			97		**Jonah**				
					3:1 – 5, 10			63	

INDEX OF READINGS

The numbers on this chart refer to sections, not to pages.

READING	A	B	C	W	READING	A	B	C	W
Micah					**Matthew (continued)**				
5:1 – 3			12		8:5 – 11				229
					8:14 – 17				530
Habakkuk					9:9 – 13	83			376
1:2 – 3; 2:2 – 4			136		9:35 – 38				508
					9:35 — 10:1, 5a, 6 – 7				173
Zephaniah					9:36 — 10:8	86			
2:3; 3:12 – 13	65				10:26 – 31	89			
3:14 – 15			9		10:40 – 42	92			
3:17 – 18a				302	11:2 – 11	7			
					11:25 – 26, 28 – 30				535
Zechariah					11:25 – 30	95			
2:14 – 15				47	11:25 – 30	164			
9:9 – 10	95				11:29 – 30				199
					13:1 – 9	98			
Malachi					13:24 – 30	101			
2:8 – 10	146				13:31 – 32				500
3:1 – 2b			252		13:44 – 46	104			200
3:19 – 20			154		13:44 – 46				495
					13:54 – 58				288
Matthew					14:13 – 21	107			
1:16, 18 – 21, 24a				272	14:22 – 33	110			415
1:18 – 24	10				14:22 – 33				201
2:1 – 12	16	16	16		15:21 – 28	113			
2:13 – 15, 19 – 23	14	14	14		16:13 – 19				319
2:13 – 18				439	16:13 – 19a				263
3:1 – 9, 11	4				16:13 – 20	116			
4:1 – 11	18				16:21 – 25	119			
4:17 – 23	62				17:1 – 9	21			344
4:18 – 22				423	18:1 – 4				473
5:1 – 12a	65			402	18:1 – 5, 10				384
5:1 – 12a				512	18:15 – 17	122			
5:1 – 12a				517	18:19 – 22				512
5:13 – 16	68			491	18:21 – 35	125			
5:14 – 16				193	20:1 – 16a	128			
5:20 – 24				180	20:26b – 28				455
5:23 – 24	71				21:1 – 11	33			
5:38 – 48	74				21:28 – 32	131			
5:43 – 48				181	21:33 – 43	134			
5:43 – 48				194	22:1 – 10	137			
6:1 – 4				176	22:15 – 21	140			
6:1 – 6, 16 – 18				176	22:34 – 40	143			
6:1, 5 – 6				176	22:35 – 40				478
6:1, 16 – 18				176	23:1 – 12	146			
6:7 – 13				195	24:37 – 44	1			
6:7 – 15				178	25:1 – 13	149			
6:19 – 21				196	25:14 – 15, 19 – 21	152			
6:24 – 34	77				25:14 – 29				202
6:25b – 33				197	25:14 – 30				495
7:1 – 5				198	25:31 – 40				177
7:7 – 11				179	25:31 – 40				473
7:21, 24 – 27				228	25:31 – 46	155			
7:21 – 27	80				27:11 – 54	33			

INDEX OF READINGS

The numbers on this chart refer to sections, not to pages.

READING	Volume A	B	C	W	READING	Volume A	B	C	W
Matthew (continued)					**Luke (continued)**				
28:16 – 20	52	159		464	1:26 – 38				429
					1:26 – 38				451
Mark					1:39 – 45			12	
1:1 – 8		5			1:39 – 56				302
1:12 – 15		19			1:39 – 56				352
1:14 – 20		63		464	1:46 – 56				175
1:21 – 28		66			2:1 – 14	13	13	13	
1:29 – 39		69			2:16 – 21	15	15	15	
1:40 – 45		72			2:22 – 32				252
2:1 – 12		75			2:41 – 51				272
2:18 – 22		78			2:41 – 51				303
2:23 – 28		81			2:41 – 51				451
3:20 – 21, 31 – 35		84			3:1a, 2 – 6			6	
3:20 – 26, 31 – 35		84			3:10 – 16, 18			9	
4:1 – 9				203	3:15 – 16, 21 – 22	17	17	17	
4:1 – 9				469	4:1 – 13			20	
4:30 – 34		87			4:14 – 21			64	
4:35 – 41		90		204	4:20b – 24, 28 – 30			67	
5:18 – 20				500	5:1 – 11			70	508
5:21 – 24, 35b – 36, 38 – 42				205	6:12 – 16				455
5:21 – 24, 35 – 43		93			6:17, 20 – 23			73	
6:1 – 6		96			6:27 – 37			76	
6:7 – 13		99			6:39 – 45			79	
6:17 – 29				365	7:1 – 10			82	210
6:30 – 34		102			7:11 – 17			85	211
7:1 – 5, 14 – 15, 21 – 23		120			7:11 – 17				535
7:31 – 37		123			7:17 – 26				174
8:31 – 35		126			7:36 – 50			88	212
9:2 – 10		22		344	9:1 – 6				192
9:33 – 37		129		206	9:1 – 6				213
9:33 – 37				473	9:11b – 17			163	
9:38 – 41		132			9:18 – 24			91	
10:13 – 16		135		207	9:28b – 36			23	344
10:13 – 16				478	9:57 – 62			94	
10:17 – 27		138			10:1 – 9			97	396
10:28 – 30				508	10:25 – 37			100	214
10:35 – 45		141			10:25 – 37				526
10:46 – 52		144		208	10:38 – 42			103	
11:1 – 10		34			11:1 – 10			106	
12:28 – 31		147			11:5 – 10				215
12:28b – 31				182	12:15 – 21				522
12:41 – 44		150		209	12:16 – 21			109	
13:24 – 32		153			12:32 – 34				473
13:33 – 37		2			12:35 – 38				172
14:12 – 16, 22 – 26		162		487	12:35 – 40			112	230
15:1 – 39		34			12:49 – 53			115	
16:15 – 18				247	13:6 – 9			26	216
16:15 – 20		53		284	13:22 – 30			118	
					14:1, 7 – 14			121	
Luke					14:12 – 14				217
1:5 – 17				316	14:25 – 27			124	
1:26 – 38		11		274	15:1 – 3, 11 – 32			29	491

The numbers on this chart refer to sections, not to pages.

Reading	A	B	C	W
Luke (continued)				
15:1 – 7				218
15:3 – 7			166	
15:11 – 32			127	
16:10 – 13			130	
16:19 – 31			133	
17:5 – 10			136	
17:11 – 19			139	219
17:11 – 19				504
17:20 – 21				231
18:1 – 8a				220
18:1 – 8			142	
18:9 – 14			145	
19:1 – 10			148	446
19:28 – 40			35	
20:27 – 38			151	
21:5 – 19			154	
21:25 – 28, 34 – 36			3	
23:1 – 49			35	
23:35 – 43			157	
24:13 – 35	40			
24:35 – 48		41		
24:50 – 53			54	
John				
1:19 – 28		8		
1:29 – 34	59			
1:35 – 42		60		
1:47 – 51				381
2:1 – 12			61	
2:13 – 22		25		
3:13 – 17				370
3:16 – 17	158	28		221
4:5 – 15, 19b – 26, 39a, 40 – 42	24			
4:46 – 53				183
6:1 – 15		105		
6:24 – 29		108		
6:48 – 51		111		
6:51 – 58	161	114		487
6:60 – 69		117		
8:1 – 11			32	
9:1, 6 – 12, 35 – 38	27			
10:1 – 10	43			
10:11 – 16		44		
10:14 – 16				190
10:27 – 30			45	
11:3 – 7, 17, 20 – 27, 31 – 45	30			
11:17 – 27				337
11:21 – 27				535
11:47 – 52				184
12:24 – 26		31		460
13:31a, 33 – 35			48	
John (continued)				
13:34 – 35				222
14:1 – 12	46			
14:12 – 14				186
14:15 – 17				223
14:15 – 17				483
14:15 – 21	49			
14:21 – 26				189
14:23 – 26			51	495
14:23 – 26				483
14:27				224
15:1 – 4				478
15:1 – 5				225
15:1 – 5, 7 – 8		47		
15:5 – 8				478
15:9 – 11				226
15:9 – 11				478
15:9 – 14			50	
15:12 – 15				227
15:18 – 21				188
15:26 — 16:1				191
16:12 – 15			160	
17:6 – 9	55			
17:11		56		
17:20 – 21			57	
17:21 – 23				187
18:33b – 37		156		
19:25 – 27				371
19:25 – 27				451
19:31 – 37		165		
20:1 – 2, 11 – 18				333
20:1 – 9	36	36	36	
20:2 – 8				438
20:11 – 18				185
20:19 – 23	58	58	58	
20:19 – 29	37	38	39	
20:24 – 29				322
21:1 – 14			42	
21:15 – 17				464
Acts				
1:8 – 11	52	53	54	
1:12 – 13a, 14				448
1:12 – 14	55			
1:15 – 17, 20a, 20c – 26		56		293
2:1 – 6, 14, 22b – 23, 32 – 33				480
2:1 – 11	58	58	58	
2:14, 22 – 24	40			
2:14a, 36 – 41	43			
2:32 – 33				185
2:42 – 47	37			484
3:1 – 10				186
3:1 – 10				452

The numbers on this chart refer to sections, not to pages.

READING	A	B	C	W
Acts (continued)				
3:13 – 15, 17 – 19		41		
4:8 – 12		44		
4:32 – 35		38		470
4:32 – 35				187
5:12 – 16			39	
5:17 – 21				188
5:27 – 32				189
5:27b – 32, 40b – 41			42	
6:1 – 7a	46			
6:8 – 10; 7:54 – 60				437
7:55 – 60			57	457
8:5 – 8, 14 – 17	49			
9:1 – 20				190
9:26 – 28		47		
10:25 – 26, 34 – 35, 44 – 48		50		
10:34 – 38	17	17	17	
10:34a, 37 – 43	36	36	36	
11:19 – 22, 26c				191
11:21 – 26; 13:1 – 3				310
11:27 – 30				177
12:1 – 11				319
13:43 – 44, 47 – 48			45	
14:21 – 27			48	
16:22 – 34				192
22:3 – 16				247
28:11 – 16				415
Romans				
1:1c – 4				274
1:2 – 4		10		
4:18 – 21		83		
5:5 – 11			166	
5:6 – 11		86		
5:10b – 11				226
6:3 – 4, 8 – 9		92		
8:9, 11		95		
8:14 – 17			159	480
8:14 – 18		98		
8:26 – 27		101		
8:28 – 30		104		
8:31, 38 – 39			22	
8:35, 37 – 39		107		
11:33 – 36		116		
12:1 – 2		119		
12:9 – 12			130	
12:9 – 16b				302
12:17 – 18, 21				181
13:8 – 10		122		
13:11 – 13a		1		
14:7 – 9		125		
15:4 – 6		4		
16:25 – 27			11	
1 Corinthians				
1:3 – 9		2		
1:10 – 13, 17	62			
1:26 – 31	65			
1:26 – 31				470
2:1 – 5	68			
2:6 – 10	71			
3:18 – 20	74			
5:6b – 8	36	36	36	
9:16 – 18		69		
10:16 – 17	161			
10:31 — 11:1		72		
11:23 – 26			163	
12:4 – 7, 12 – 13	58	58	58	
12:4 – 11			61	
12:4 – 13				480
12:12 – 13				225
12:12 – 13				475
12:12 – 14, 27			64	
13:4 – 7				194
13:4 – 8a, 11 – 13			67	
13:4 – 13				470
15:3 – 8, 11			70	
15:12, 16 – 20			73	
15:20 – 24a	155			
2 Corinthians				
1:3 – 4				175
4:6 – 11		81		
4:16 — 5:1		84		
5:6 – 10		87		
5:14 – 17		90		
5:17 – 19			29	
6:4 – 10				457
8:1 – 3a, 12				209
8:7, 9, 13 – 14		93		
9:8 – 11				519
12:7 – 10		96		
13:11 – 13	158			
Galatians				
1:11 – 12, 15 – 19			85	
3:26 – 28				475
3:26 – 29			91	
5:1, 13 – 15			94	
5:22 – 23, 25 – 26				223
Ephesians				
1:3 – 5				532
1:3 – 6				448
1:3 – 10		99		
1:15 – 16a, 18 – 19a				205

INDEX OF READINGS

The numbers on this chart refer to sections, not to pages.

Reading	A	B	C	W
Ephesians (continued)				
1:17 – 21	52	53	54	
2:4 – 10		28		
2:20 – 22				443
2:20 – 22				452
3:14 – 19		165		
3:16b – 17, 20 – 21				231
4:1 – 6		105		
4:1 – 7				466
4:11 – 13				466
4:31 — 5:2		111		
5:1 – 2, 8 – 10	27			488
5:8 – 10				193
5:15 – 20		114		
6:1 – 4		117		
6:18b – 19a, 20b				220
Philippians				
1:4 – 6			6	
2:1 – 5	131			
3:12 – 14			32	
3:20 — 4:1			23	
4:4 – 7			9	230
4:4 – 9				470
4:6 – 9	134			514
4:8 – 9				199
4:12 – 14, 19 – 20	137			
Colossians				
1:15 – 18			157	
1:18 – 20			100	
1:27 – 28			103	
2:6 – 7				216
3:1 – 2				196
3:1 – 4	36	36	36	
3:1 – 4			109	
3:12 – 13				198
3:12 – 14				178
3:12 – 15				514
3:12, 15b – 17				497
3:12 – 17	14	14	14	
3:15 – 16				224
3:17, 23 – 24				288
1 Thessalonians				
1:1 – 5b	140			
1:5 – 8a	143			
2:7 – 9, 13	146			
4:13 – 14, 18				532
4:13 – 18	149			
5:1 – 6	152			
5:16 – 18				219
5:16 – 24			8	

Reading	A	B	C	W
2 Thessalonians				
1:11 – 12			148	
2:16 — 3:5			151	
3:6 – 12, 16				492
3:7 – 12			154	
1 Timothy				
1:12 – 15b			127	
2:1 – 4				195
6:11b – 12a			133	
2 Timothy				
1:6 – 8			136	
1:1 – 8				248
2:11 – 13			139	
4:1 – 2			142	
4:6 – 8			145	
4:17 – 18				319
Titus				
1:1 – 5				248
3:4 – 6	13	13	13	
Hebrews				
4:12 – 13		138		
4:14 – 16		141		
5:1 – 6		144		
7:26		147		
11:1 – 2, 8 – 12			112	
12:1 – 4			115	
12:5a, 6 – 7, 11			118	
13:1 – 3, 14 – 16				523
James				
1:17 – 18, 21b – 22		120		
2:1 – 5		123		
2:14 – 17				228
2:14 – 17				488
2:14 – 18		126		217
3:17 – 18		129		
5:1 – 6		132		
5:7 – 10	7			
5:13 – 16				527
5:16b – 18				215
1 Peter				
1:3 – 4	37			200
2:9 – 10				222
4:7b – 11				470
4:10 – 11				202
4:13 – 16	55			
5:1 – 4				263
5:12 – 14				284

The numbers on this chart refer to sections, not to pages.

READING	Volume			
	A	B	C	W
2 Peter				
1:16 – 19				344
1 John				
2:29b — 3:1a				206
3:1, 23				227
3:1 – 2		44		532
3:11, 18				214
3:16 – 18				470
3:18		47		
4:7 – 10		50		212
4:7 – 11, 16b	164			
4:11 – 13		56		
5:1 – 3		38		
5:2 – 5				470
Revelation				
1:5 – 8		156		
7:9 – 10				402
12:7 – 12a				381
14:13				532
21:1 – 4			48	443
21:1 – 8				488
21:10 – 14, 22 – 23			51	